AN INTRODUCTION TO
PAINTING THE NUDE

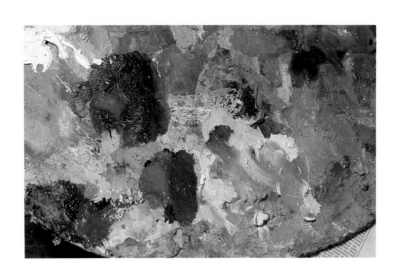

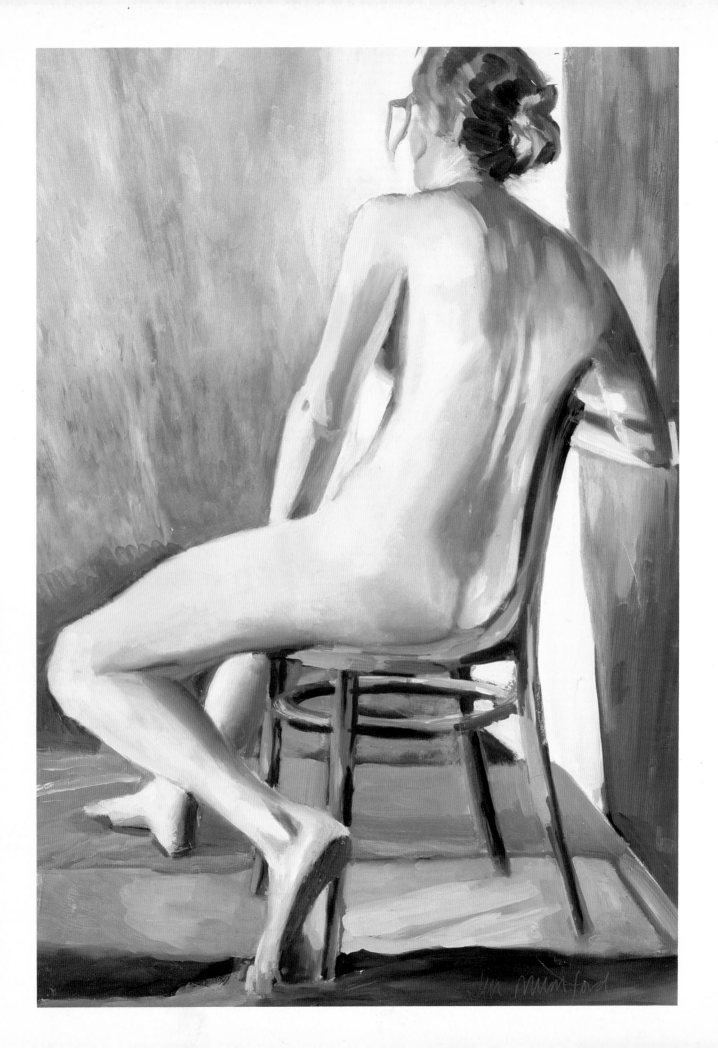

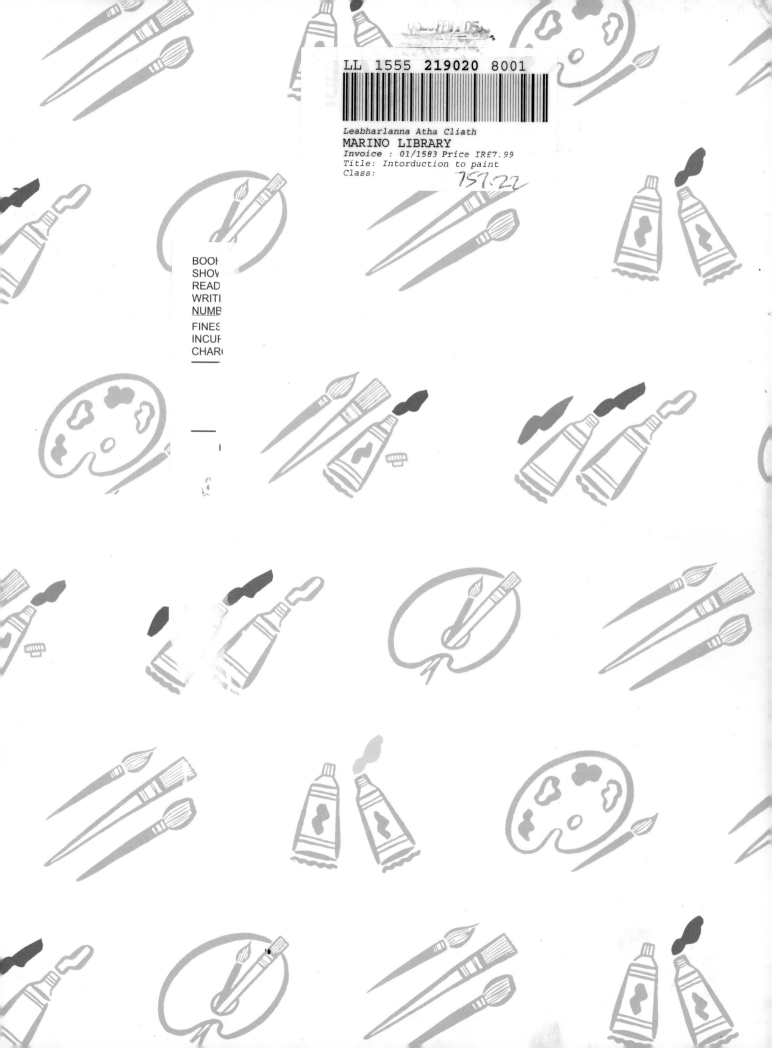

AN INTRODUCTION TO
PAINTING THE NUDE

ANATOMY · FORM · COMPOSITION · TONE · STRUCTURE · COLOR

DAVID CARR

CHARTWELL
BOOKS, INC.

A QUINTET BOOK

Published by Chartwell Books
A Division of Book Sales, Inc.
110 Enterprise Avenue
Secaucus, New Jersey 07094

This edition produced for sale
in the U.S.A., its territories
and dependencies only.

ISBN 1-55521-902-0

This book was designed and produced by
Quintet Publishing Limited
6 Blundell Street
London N7 9BH

Creative Director: Richard Dewing
Designer: Ian Hunt
Project Editor: Helen Denholm
Editor: Helen Douglas-Cooper
Photographers: Paul Forrester, Martin Norris

Typeset in Great Britain by
Central Southern Typesetters, Eastbourne
Manufactured in Hong Kong by Regent Publishing Services Limited
Printed in Hong Kong by Leefung-Asco Printers Limited

PICTURE CREDITS

Page 9: *Bathsheba with King David's Letter* by
Rembrandt van Rijn, Edimedia Photographic
Agency, Paris.

Page 78: *Annette Assise* (1954) by Alberto
Giacometti © ADAGP, Paris and DACS,
London, 1993.

With special thanks to Russell & Chapple Ltd,
suppliers of artists' canvases and artists'
materials, for providing brushes and canvas for
photography.

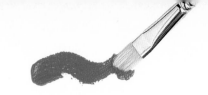

CONTENTS

INTRODUCTION 6

1 GENERAL INFORMATION ON OILS AND WATERCOLORS 11

2 SEEING THINGS SIMPLY 19

3 COMPOSING A PICTURE 26

4 ALLA PRIMA TECHNIQUE 32

5 SEEING PLANES AND STRUCTURE 40

6 ANATOMY 46

7 HEAD, NECK, AND SHOULDERS 52

8 THE FACE AND ITS FEATURES 58

9 ARMS, HANDS, AND FEET 61

10 SKIN COLOR AND TONE 68

11 TWO APPROACHES TO PAINTING THE FIGURE 74

12 TONAL PAINTING 80

13 LIGHT AND COLOR 84

14 OIL GLAZE TECHNIQUE 97

15 WATERCOLOR GLAZE TECHNIQUE 104

16 WET-INTO-WET WATERCOLOR 112

17 TAKING IT FURTHER 117

INDEX 128

INTRODUCTION

The portrayal of the human figure has been an abiding concern of artists from the earliest times to the present day. Despite the trend towards abstraction, their fascination with the figure has not diminished in the 20th century, and the nude continues to occupy a central place in contemporary art. The statement made by the 18th-century English poet Alexander Pope – "The proper study of mankind is man" – is as true today as it was for earlier societies.

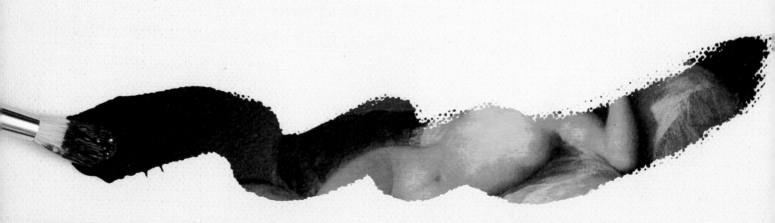

Naturally enough, in visual terms the human form has performed a large variety of different functions through the centuries. The scientific study of the nude – and of anatomy – is essentially an innovation of the Renaissance. Nonetheless, without acute observational skills prehistoric artists would not have been able to depict running and hunting figures with such eloquence. For them, function – the magical power over prey – dictated style (if they depicted a speared antelope, such would be the outcome of their hunting). The famous Willendorf Venus shows a rotund female form with large breasts, and was a symbol of fertility. In the exotic art of India the hips and breasts are exaggerated.

Art is created out of that tension between the natural (retinal) appearance of things and society's needs and influences, as well as from the artist's feelings and

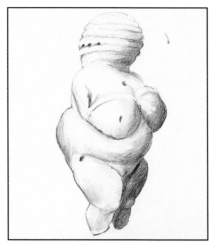

A B O V E **A pencil study of the *Venus of Willendorf*, one of the earliest known pieces of prehistoric sculpture: a small fertility image of Palæolithic origin dating from around 30,000–25,000 BC. At first sight it appears oversimplified and stylized, but in drawing it one realizes just how well the form has been observed. It repays study to make copies of works of art of all periods.**

B E L O W **Egyptian art existed to glorify the pharoahs and the noble classes. Their highly stylized paintings were governed by strict rules, ensuring that every feature was shown to the best advantage.**

emotions, and is frequently a complex mixture of all three. In earlier societies the artists' personality tends to be less obvious, and it is perhaps only since Renaissance times that the artist assumes increasing importance. We have a story of changing ideas and requirements.

In Ancient Egypt a strict formal imagery was imposed upon artists in describing daily life, and the way of death and after-life. Their art would not work, however, without a strong observational base and, as art historian E. H. Gombrich suggests, their figures are presented to us with each element shown to best advantage and from its most characteristic angle: the head in profile but with a full face; the shoulders and chest from the front; the stomach, legs and feet from the side. We have to wait for Pablo Picasso (1881–1973) to find such inventive distortion again.

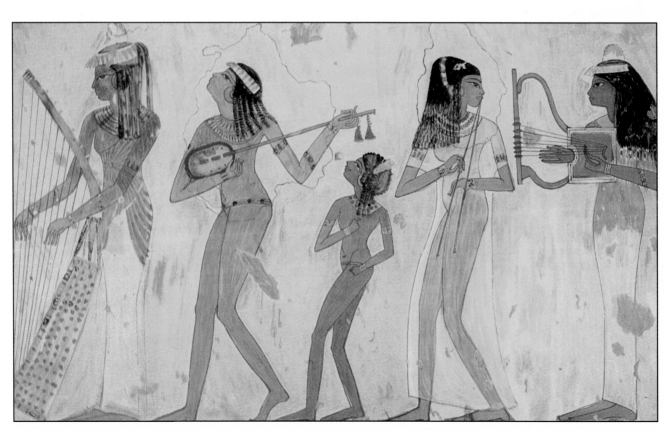

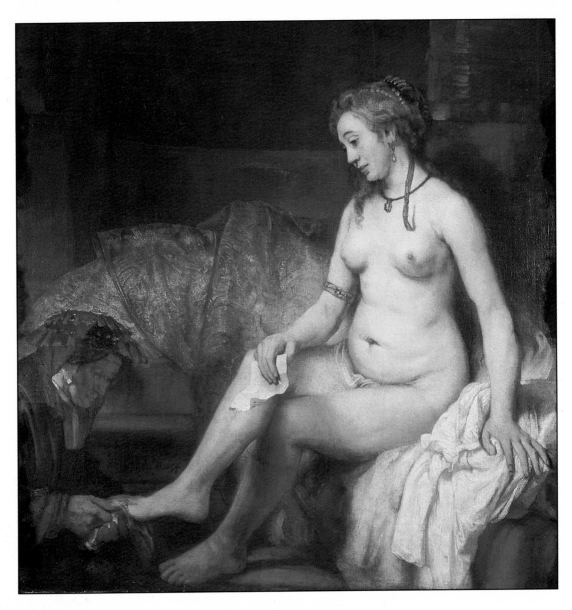

Greek art displays a much more naturalistic ideal of beauty, based on a sound knowledge of human form, but it is nonetheless an ideal and in that sense formalized. It was here, and later with the Romans, that some of the formal archetypes (e.g., the Capitoline Venus and the Three Graces) appear and reappear throughout the history of art. The Romans, the Etruscans, and the wall-paintings of Pompeii show a real grasp of form and space.

Observational skills lay dormant throughout most of the Middle Ages, but pictorial storytelling flourished at the behest of the

ABOVE **The model for Rembrandt's** ***Bathsheba with King David's Letter*** **(1654) was his common-law wife, Hendrickje Stoffels. He created a whole world in his studio where models and sitters reenacted life under his direction. Based not so much on the art of the past as on Rembrandt's own experience, this powerful figure is more personal and intimate than anything we might expect to find during the Renaissance, except perhaps in Titian.**

church. Imagery became transcendental and hierarchical. Much expressive and highly charged work appeared during the later Gothic period, and the figure was used in a way that emerged again in 20th-century Expressionist art.

With the growth of humanism and the reawakening of people's interest in their life on earth, with St. Francis's reverence for things physical and earthly, and the emergence of a real scientific interest in man and his world we reach the Renaissance. The great classical traditions come alive again, and in the space of 250 years we move from the monumental form

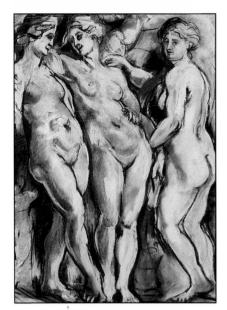

A B O V E *The Three Graces* is of Greek origin and was copied by the Romans. A Pompeiian wall-painting of the 1st century AD depicts them. In the 18th century Antonio Canova (1757–1822) produced his famous group, and in the 20th century the sculptor Maillol has used the theme. Rubens was one of many painters to employ this archetype in his work, and this charcoal drawing by the author is based on a small sepia oil sketch by Rubens.

and space of Giotto (1266?–1337) and Masaccio (1401–28), through Leonardo da Vinci (1452–1519) and Michelangelo (1475–1564), to the riotous extravagance of the Baroque and Rococo periods in the 17th and early 18th centuries. The great religious themes of the Crucifixion and Deposition, where human beings gather around the dead Christ, attain increasing realism.

These religious and mythological themes and classical archetypes find their northern expression with Peter Paul Rubens (1577–1640). He is further recorded as having made notes on color theory, and the subtle rainbow colors in his treatment of flesh find a later flowering in the work of Eugène Delacroix (1798–1863) and Auguste Renoir (1841–1919). Arguably, work of the deepest humanity is found in Rubens's contemporary, Rembrandt van Rijn (1606–69), who made constant use of models in his work. One of the most tangible, authoritative and real nudes in Western painting appears in his *Bathsheba with King David's Letter*.

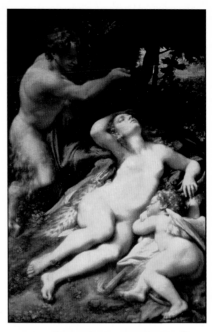

A B O V E Correggio, a contemporary of Titian, was a masterly painter of light flowing over soft and graceful form, as can be seen in his *Jupiter and Antiope* (c 1531). Equally at home with religious or mythological subjects, he makes his Antiope as seductive as possible under the approaching Jupiter.

B E L O W Goya painted the *Naked Maja* (*Maja Desnuda* – the Spanish *maja* meaning "a flirt") around 1798, the subject being the Duchess of Alba, a close friend and by all accounts the mistress of the artist. There is, of course, an equally famous version of Her Grace clothed.

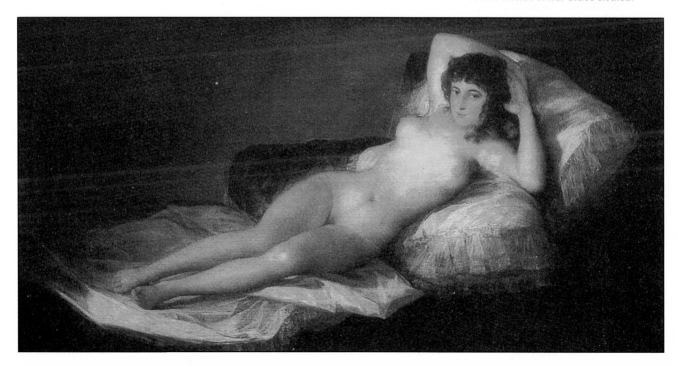

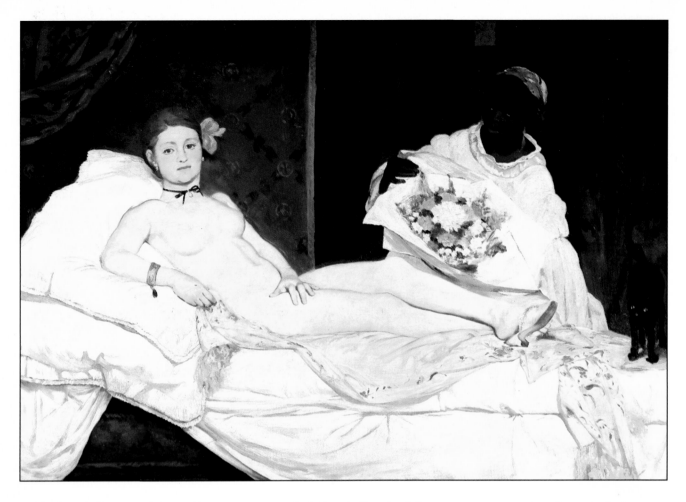

The female form is celebrated by Giorgione (1478–1510) and Titian (1485?–1576) in the 15th and 16th centuries, with their classically posed and sumptuous Venuses, and frequently by Correggio (1489?–1534) within a framework of classical subject matter. But perhaps it is only with Francisco Goya (1746–1828) and his *Naked Maja* that the nude stares at us, unabashed, and in the 19th century, *Olympia* by Edouard Manet (1832–83) faces us with her implacable look, coolly gazing at the observer from her huge satin bed.

The life room, where artists and students gathered to study formally the male and female figures, is a relatively recent phenomenon, dating back to the 18th century, and a rich tradition has developed from it. Many 20th-century artists have broken the mold of classical

A B O V E **Both Manet's *Olympia* (1863), illustrated here, and Goya's *Maja Desnuda* on page 9 are variations on the theme of the Renaissance classical model. Manet's model comes at the end of a long line of Venuses. The classical reclining nude rediscovered by Giorgione and Titian was brought right up to date in Manet's avowedly realist approach, which employed a real model in a situation that scandalized people at the time.**

representation. From the intimate domestic settings of Pierre Bonnard (1867–1947), the light and color of the "odalisques" of Henri Matisse (1869–1954) to the inventive and authoritative forms of Picasso, the figure has been an unending source of inspiration and variety. Northern artists, meanwhile – Edvard Munch (1863–1944), Max Beckmann (1884–1950) or the German Expressionists, for example – have used the figure to reflect and comment upon the human condition.

In the work of Balthus (*b* 1908), Alberto Giacometti (1901–66), Richard Diebenkorn (*b* 1922) and Francis Bacon (1909–92) we find artists of the late 20th century continuing the great figurative tradition. With the nude as a central element in their art, they produce images for our time.

1

GENERAL INFORMATION ON OILS AND WATERCOLORS

The wonderful colors that we use are made from pigments held together by a binding vehicle. In the case of oil paints the vehicle is cold-pressed or refined linseed oil, or sometimes poppy oil. The water-based fresco painting of southern Italy suffered badly in more northern climes, and gradually oil painting came into its own for artistic purposes around the early 15th century in Northern Europe, and shortly after that in Venice. It began to be widely used by Flemish artists as the demand and preference for a new type of easel painting developed. During the following 200 years it gained gradual acceptance, especially among the later Italian painters, and by the 17th century its use had become common.

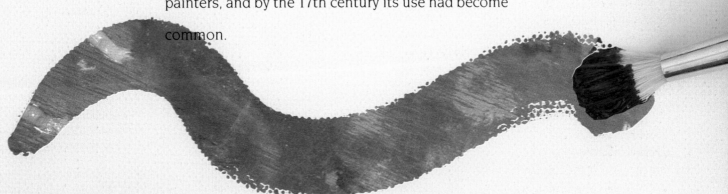

Watercolor employs almost all the same dry pigment colors as oil paint, but they are ground in gum arabic, which is water soluble. Watercolor painting as a distinct technique was not employed much before the 18th century, when the English school firmly established its practice. Watercolor paintings dry by evaporation (of the water), leaving the pigment stuck to the paper by the gum. Oil paints, on the other hand, "saponify": the air causes the oil to undergo a chemical change, gradually becoming more "soapy" and ultimately becoming a tough paint film.

It is not true that watercolors fade more quickly than oils because of their relatively thin film of color. Kept away from direct and bright light, they have as long a life as oil paintings, which in any case should also be displayed away from bright light.

Students' or artists' quality?

There is a choice between students' quality and artists' quality paint. There is only one possible reason for buying students' quality, and that is an economic one. These paints are characterized by a uniformly low price. Consequently the more expensive pigments (such as cadmiums) will be replaced by substitute approximations and labelled cadmium red (hue). They often contain extenders, neutral-colored substances that bulk out the paint, whereas artists' quality paints contain pure pigment.

Obviously, if you are starting out and need to buy a large number of colors, it is a help financially to buy students' quality paints, but you should replace them with artists' quality as soon as you can afford to. Ultimately, it is a false economy to buy students' quality as you will use far more paint trying to achieve the brilliance that you can get with a small amount of artists' quality, just as a good-quality brush outlasts several cheaper ones.

Students' quality paints often have a brand name as well as the manufacturer's name, and will all be the same price. Artists' quality paints must be labelled *Artists' oil color* or *Artists' watercolor*, and the price will vary with the pigment. Earth colors will be cheapest, cadmiums and cobalts the most expensive. (Beware one paint firm that states on its students' quality paints *Oil color for artists* – this is *not* artists' oil color.)

Now we come to the palette – not the one on which we mix our colors (more of that later), but meaning the range of colors we use. A bewildering number of colors are available, but many are unnecessary except in the case of individual needs or preferences, which come with experience. Picasso said, "Actually, you work with only a few colors, but they seem like a lot more when each is in the right place." Rembrandt used yellow, warm browns and reds, a blue pigment called smalt, an occasional green, black and white. Rubens and Titian used very few more, and Monet, that great painter of light, used a palette restricted to white, emerald green, cobalt blue, *garance toncée* (burnt madder), and chrome yellow.

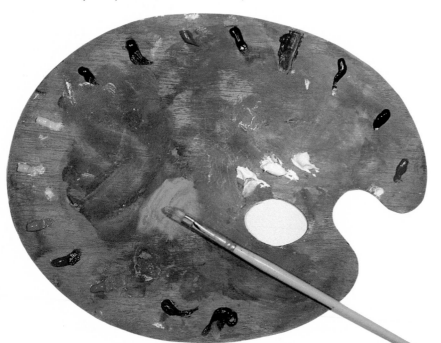

LEFT A competent pianist does not have to search for the notes on the keyboard, and no more should we have to search for our colors. A system that makes sense is based on the color circle (see page 85). Starting at the top right and moving counterclockwise: violet, French ultramarine, cobalt blue, cerulean blue, Prussian blue, cobalt green, viridian green, raw umber, cadmium lemon, cadmium yellow mid, yellow ocher, burnt sienna, cadmium red, mars red, alizarin crimson, and titanium white. There are one or two optional extra colors here: cobalt green, burnt sienna and mars red, and they have been given a relevant position on the palette. The colors move from violet into warm (i.e. violet) blues, into cold (i.e. green) blues and green, then cold yellows, becoming warmer and moving through yellow ocher to hot yellows and red, and finally through cold red (crimson) back around to violet.

MATERIALS FOR OIL PAINTING

The following is a basic recommended list of oil colors: French ultramarine, cobalt blue, cerulean or manganese blue, (phthalo or Prussian blue), (cobalt green), viridian green, raw umber, cadmium lemon or cadmium pale, cadmium yellow mid, yellow ocher, (raw sienna), (light red), cadmium red, alizarin crimson, violet, and titanium white.

A violet is useful, but in artists' quality cobalt violet is extremely expensive, so look for a substitute. The colors in parenthesis are useful but not essential. Black has been omitted at this stage because when used to darken colors it usually only makes them dirty.

The basic shape of the palette is unimportant. What is important is to have a system for laying out colors. Firstly they should be placed around the edges of the palette to allow maximum space for mixing and to facilitate cleaning afterwards, leaving unused paint around the edge. There is nothing worse than a palette with paint randomly squeezed all over it with no sequence at all. Painting is demanding enough without adding to the problem.

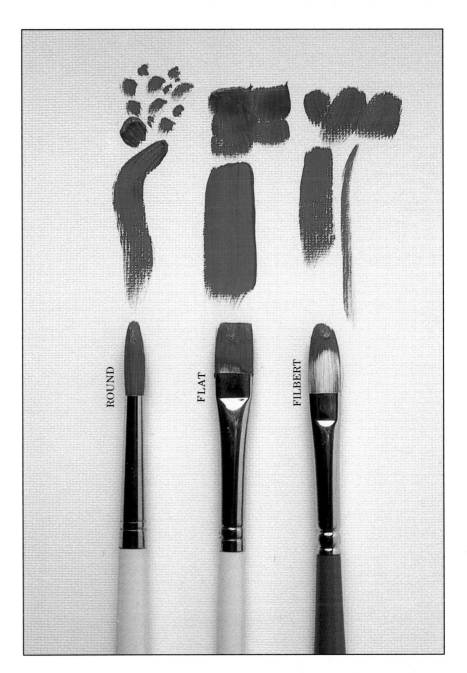

ROUND

FLAT

FILBERT

ABOVE **The three basic shapes of brush used for painting in oils, and the marks they make.**

Brushes

Brushes for oil should be hog-hair, and come in a range of shapes and sizes. It is a false economy to purchase cheap brushes; they lose their shape quickly and become limp. There are three basic shapes – round, square, and filbert. I would recommend the filbert as the best all-purpose brush. It can be used flat to cover large areas, on its edge for linear work, or its point for fine detail. A small round brush is a help for linear work. Long-handled sables can be useful for very fine detail. A no. 5 and a no. 8 filbert are versatile enough for most occasions.

Palette

A palette can be purchased ready made, and the strip-off disposable types are also useful. However, it is recommended that you make your own simply by giving the smooth side of a piece of hardboard or composition board a coat of clear varnish and allowing it to dry overnight.

Mediums

White spirit for cleaning brushes as you proceed, and genuine turpentine for mixing with the paint, are all that you need. You should purchase these from a general or hardware store as they are the same as the more expensive versions sold in art stores. Refined linseed oil for mixing with the paint in the later stages of a picture must be purchased from art stores. A useful all-purpose painting medium is a 50/50 mixture of genuine turpentine and linseed oil.

Supports

Wood Plywood tends to warp and separate. Blockboard is solid, but heavy. Hardboard can generally be recommended, but use the smooth side. The textured side does not approximate to canvas – it blots up the paint and ruins the brushes. Some hardboard now produced is smooth on both sides. Larger pieces will need a batten support at the back. MDF (medium density fiber board) is one of the best and most inert surfaces now available, and comes in various thicknesses.

Oil painting paper and canvas boards These are very convenient, but the priming tends to be unpleasant and slippery to paint on.

Canvas Ready-made canvases are expensive, and it is worth the time and effort to make your own. Cotton should be avoided as it is very susceptible to changes of humidity. It slackens and tightens constantly and disturbs the ground and paint film. Linen is best, and the various grades for artistic purposes are usually available from specialized sail and canvas suppliers.

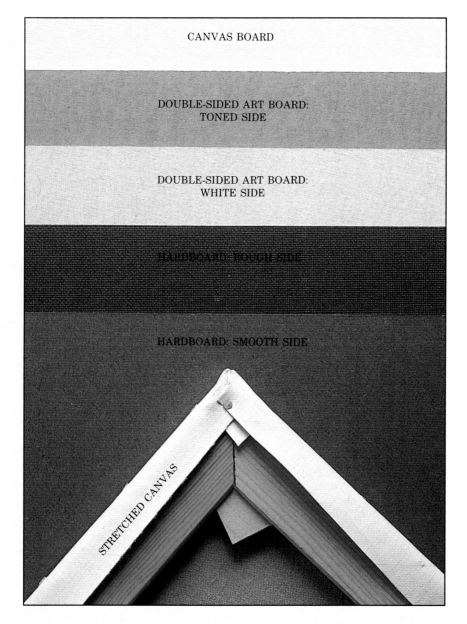

CANVAS BOARD

DOUBLE-SIDED ART BOARD: TONED SIDE

DOUBLE-SIDED ART BOARD: WHITE SIDE

HARDBOARD: ROUGH SIDE

HARDBOARD: SMOOTH SIDE

STRETCHED CANVAS

LEFT **A variety of painting surfaces for oils.**

Stretching a canvas

Canvas is normally sold by the meter or yard in large widths. Its thickness is defined by weight, so that 15 oz (510 gsm) canvas is thicker than 12 oz (410 gsm). To stretch the canvas you require stretcher bars, which can be purchased in various sizes or ordered to your own requirements from specialized woodworkers.

Priming

Boards and canvases must be primed before working in oils. It is especially true in the case of canvas, because oil in contact with bare canvas will rot it. Acrylic primers are available which do not require any prior sizing. They are adequate for boards or even paper (a good-quality matt white water-based paint is also adequate). To produce the best surface, however, you should first size the board or canvas, and then prime it with an oil-based or tempera primer.

Glue size should be purchased from good art stores. Rabbit-skin glue is the best type available. Take approximately 1 oz (25 g) dry weight and add it to 1¼ pt (600 ml) of cold water. Leave it to soak overnight. Using a double-boiler or one saucepan inside another, warm up the mixture until the glue is thoroughly dispersed. Never apply direct heat or allow the glue to boil. When the size has reached blood temperature, apply it to the board or canvas with gentle, even strokes. Do not overbrush and create bubbles. In the case of canvas, the moisture will further stretch the canvas on drying, and this is why it is important that the canvas is not too tight in the first place. Wedges should never be inserted into the stretcher corners initially, but should be used to take up slack when the picture is finished.

HOW TO STRETCH CANVAS

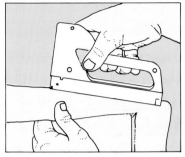

1 The tools required are a ruler, a knife, a staple gun and staples (or tacks if you prefer), and a pair of canvas pliers.

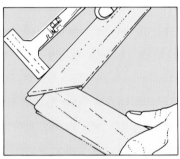

2 Fit the corners of the stretcher firmly together. Give each a sharp tap to be certain it is secure.

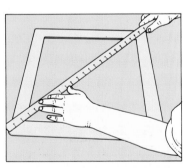

3 Check that the stretcher is square by measuring the diagonals.

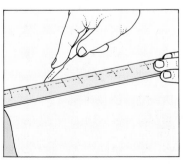

4 Cut the canvas to size using a ruler and a knife. Allow a 1½-in (3.75-cm) overlap all round.

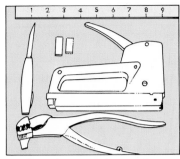

5 Lay the stretcher on the canvas. Fold the canvas over at one end and insert a staple in the outer edge of the stretcher.

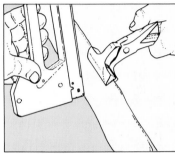

6 Use the pliers to pull the canvas tight at the opposite end, and insert a staple. Pull the other sides tight and staple.

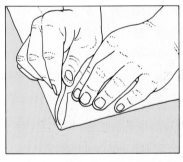

7 Insert staples at 3-in (7½-cm) intervals all around, to within 2 in (5 cm) of the corners. Fold in the first corner tightly.

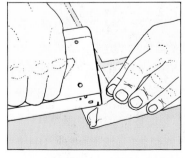

8 Secure the corner with two staples, and repeat the process for the three other corners.

Allow this coat of size to dry, ideally overnight, and the board or canvas is ready for priming. An oil-based, commercially prepared primer can be used. Alternatively, use the recipe below for a universal tempera primer for canvas, board or paper; it has proved very durable.

Take an egg and beat it thoroughly in a glass jar. Add an equal quantity of linseed oil, and beat thoroughly.

Add an equal quantity of water, and again beat thoroughly. The quantities therefore are: one part egg, one part linseed oil, and two parts water. The order in which they are mixed is crucial. The egg is an emulsifying agent, allowing oil and water to mix.

Now take some titanium white dry pigment and add it into the mixture gradually, stirring thoroughly with a spatula. The resulting mixture should have a buttery consistency and, when spread out flat with the spatula, should glisten slightly. Finally, take a very few drops of warm glue size and add it to the mixture until it is of a brushable consistency. Now prime your canvas or board with it. The result will be a technically sound priming. It is slightly absorbent, a good property for the first layers of paint.

MATERIALS FOR WATERCOLOR

Any list of watercolors approximates to that of oils. Colors can vary from firm to firm, and in the list below cobalt green dark and light and *stil de grain* pink are Schmincke, whereas aureolin and alizarin crimson are from Winsor and Newton. Only trial and error will enable you to find the exact colors you like. A comprehensive list of watercolors would include French ultramarine, cobalt blue, cerulean blue/manganese blue or equivalent, phthalo blue or Prussian blue, cobalt green dark, cobalt green light, viridian green, *stil de grain* pink or aureolin, cadmium lemon or pale, cadmium yellow mid, cadmium red light, alizarin crimson, and ultramarine violet. If you are painting with a pure watercolor technique there is no need for Chinese white.

Whether to purchase tubes or pans is largely a personal question. Pans enable you to work with greater immediacy without the nuisance of opening tubes. Tubes are useful when a large quantity of one color is needed, or when laying down a wash. You can purchase empty watercolor boxes and fill them with the colors of your choice.

Brushes

The same advice applies to water-color brushes as to oil painting brushes. It is a false economy to purchase cheap brushes. With watercolor, the inadequacies of cheap brushes are even more glaring. There is nothing more frustrating than a flaccid brush that will not make and keep a point. Sable, therefore, should be used if at all possible. There are now quite adequate sable and synthetic fiber mix brushes available that are reasonably inexpensive. Test a brush for its "spring" to see if it is any good. A good brush should have a degree of resistance.

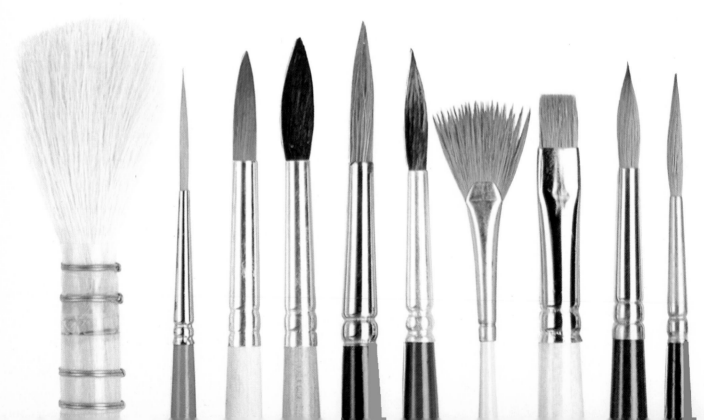

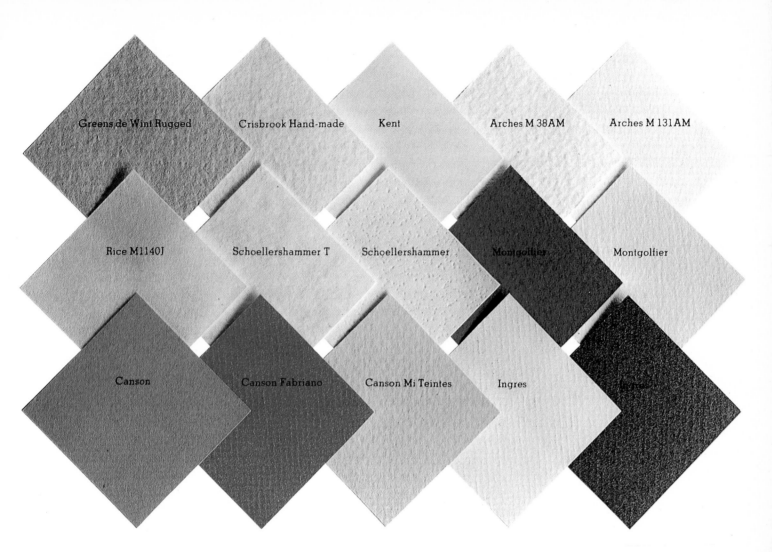

Greens de Wint Rugged • Crisbrook Hand-made • Kent • Arches M 38AM • Arches M 131AM

Rice M1140J • Schoellershammer T • Schoellershammer • Montgolfier • Montgolfier

Canson • Canson Fabriano • Canson Mi Teintes • Ingres • Ingres

Paper

The three main types of paper in use are classified as: *hot-pressed* (HP), which is smooth; *"not"* or *cold-pressed* (CP), which is lightly textured; and rough, which has a coarse-textured surface. "Not" or cold-pressed is the most popular. Its semi-rough surface takes washes well; a dryish brush dragged quickly across the surface will exploit its texture to good effect, especially at the beginning of a picture.

Paper thickness is expressed by weight. In imperial it is the weight of one ream (500 sheets; in metric, it is the weight in grams of one square meter of paper. The three most common weights are: 90 lb (185 gsm), moderately thick; 140 lb (300 gsm), thick; and 300 lb (640 gsm), almost card.

The best paper has a high rag content, ideally 100% cotton. There are many good cheaper papers available: always look for those described as wood-free.

Papers that are 90 lb (185 gsm) and 140 lb (300 gsm) will need stretching prior to use to avoid cockling, where the paint becomes uneven and can lie in puddles.

LEFT A variety of watercolor brushes. From left to right: large mop brush useful for washes, long thin rigger brush for fine lines, synthetic round hair, mixed fiber round, ox-hair round, squirrel-hair round, sable fan bright, long-handled square sable, sable round, and sable rigger.

ABOVE Some of the many different types of watercolor paper available.

HOW TO STRETCH PAPER

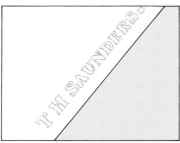

1 First check which is the right side of the paper. Hold it to the light so the watermark appears the right way around.

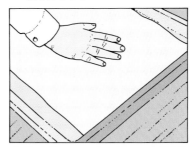

3 Soak the paper in a tray or sink full of clean water. The amount of time needed to soak varies with the type of paper.

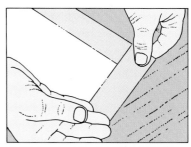

6 Stick gum strip along the opposite side of the paper. Tape the other two sides. Keep the paper absolutely flat throughout.

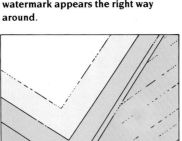

2 Trim the paper to size for the drawing board, leaving a good margin of board so that the gummed tape will adhere.

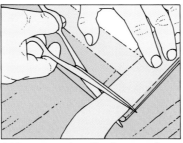

4 Measure out lengths of gummed paper tape to match each side of the drawing board.

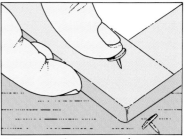

7 To secure the paper, push a thumbtack into the board at each corner. Let the paper dry naturally or it may split.

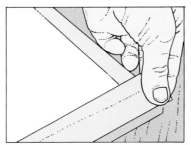

5 Take the paper out of the water and drain it off. Lay it on the board and stick dampened, gummed tape along one side.

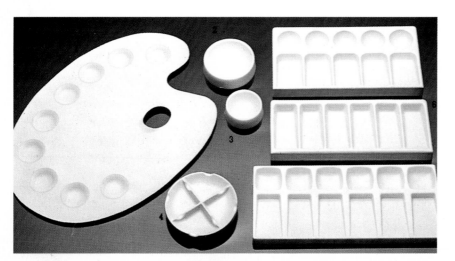

LEFT A selection of some types of palettes you can purchase for watercolors.

2

SEEING THINGS SIMPLY

Beginning to paint means beginning to *think* like a painter. The brush can move paint around and manipulate form and space, which is not the same as drawing lines and filling them in or making shapes and coloring them in. With a few strokes the brush can cover large areas of paper or canvas; just one stroke of the brush can describe, say, a whole arm or leg.

It is important to be selective in your approach to a painting. When you are confronted by a jumble of appearances, you need to make some kind of order out of the chaos. Details that might catch the eye are not as important in the early stages of a painting as developing a feeling for the whole. This process of moving from the general to the particular was well described by Eugène Delacroix when he said, "I begin with a broom and finish with a needle."

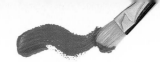

GIRL SEATED SIDEWAYS

D A V I D   C A R R

Small pieces of board and a minimum palette are used here to make two quick oil studies. The artist's aim is to see and keep things as simple as possible. The palette used consists of French ultramarine, cerulean blue, viridian green, cadmium lemon, cadmium yellow, cadmium red, alizarin crimson and titanium white, thinned with turpentine in the early stages. The brushes are a no. 5 filbert and a no. 2 round hoghair. The boards are 10 × 11 in (25 × 27.5 cm), primed with commercial primer.

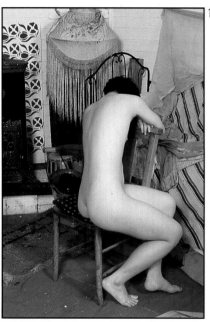

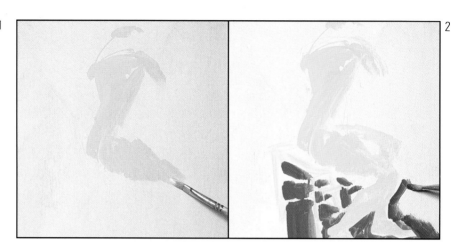

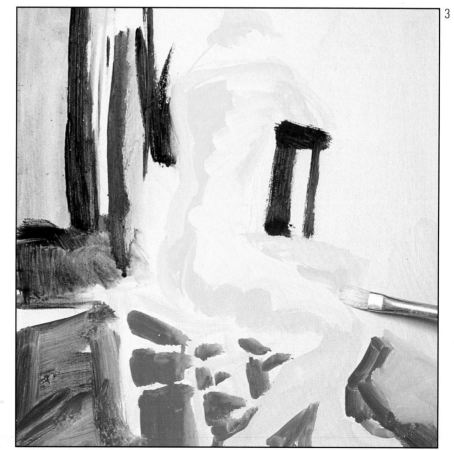

1 The model is seated sideways with her arms on the back of the chair.

2 The painter takes some cadmium yellow and, keeping the paint fairly dilute, uses the no. 5 brush to block in the figure. No linear drawing has been done. Instead, the figure is seen as a flat shape. The chair is also realized by the flat shapes around it painted in cadmium red.

3 Further shapes are placed around the figure using ultramarine and alizarin. The whole painting takes on the appearance of a flat, jigsaw puzzle arrangement of interlocking shapes. At this point some simplified form is introduced on the figure using cadmium yellow mixed with white.

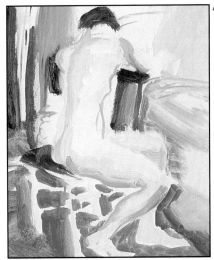

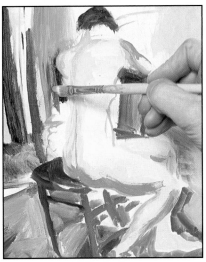

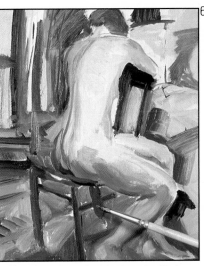

4 Some of the darker tones of the figure are now established using very light touches of light green and blue painted into the wet yellow paint. Note that the defining line down the front of the figure is put in after the main shape of the figure has been established. It was not drawn first and filled in.

5 Depth is now given to the space around the figure through variations in tone, and some of the warmer shadows on the figure, notably under the thigh, are painted in.

6 The space is pushed back and pulled forward using cool and warm colors. Ultramarine is painted into the crimson carpet, and shapes adjacent to the figure are defined. The result is a clear, simple statement.

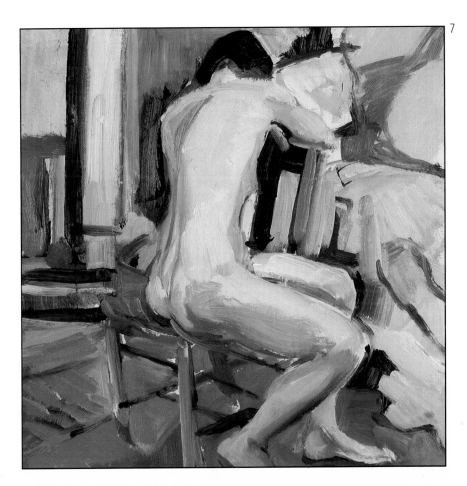

7 Every part of the picture surface has been made to work, and the figure, simply conceived, occupies a credible space.

GIRL SEATED ON ARM OF CHAIR

DAVID CARR

This is a slightly less successful attempt than the preceding example on page 20.
Nonetheless, it aptly illustrates the point. Here the length of the vertical pose
suggests a different-shaped board is required.

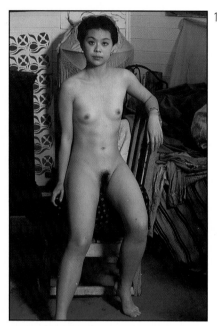

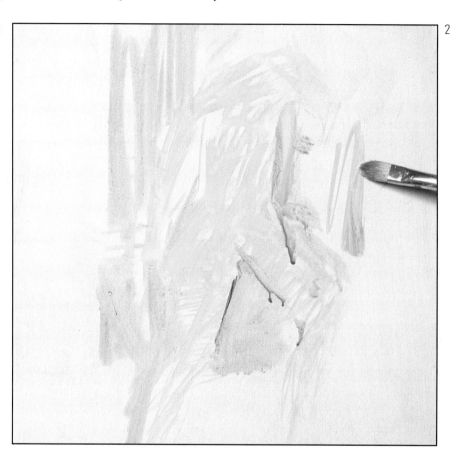

1 The model is half-seated sideways on
the arm of a chair.

2 Notice again the simple, direct approach
of lightly massing in the figure and space
with thin paint.

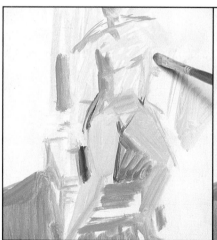
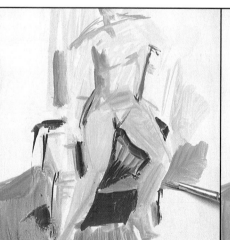
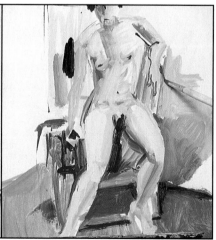

3 The artist gradually develops the shapes
around the figure. The axis of the
shoulders, breasts, and pelvis is well felt.

Note how the picture evolves through a
combination of line and mass and not
through an initial line drawing,

subsequently filled in. It is useful to think
in terms of an interlocking jigsaw puzzle of
shapes.

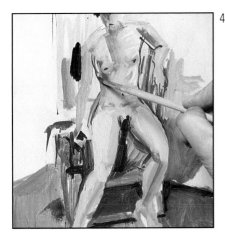

4 Into these simple areas the painter now draws with a fine brush. The figure's right side and left arm are carefully described by the shapes around them.

5 The no. 5 filbert is used again to work back into the figure more broadly. Here much of the cool lemon color of the flesh is stated.

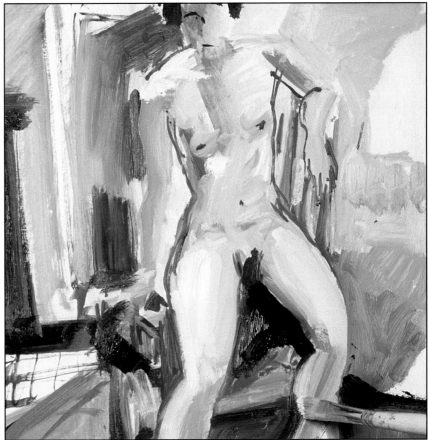

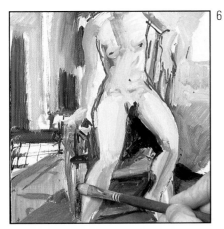

6 The space around the figure is now more thoroughly blocked in and unified.

7 Stronger defining lines are painted boldly around the legs of the figure and the seat of the chair. The head and shoulders are resolved, and although some of the top of the head and the lower foot are lost, this is a very useful preparatory study that could lead to a more finished painting.

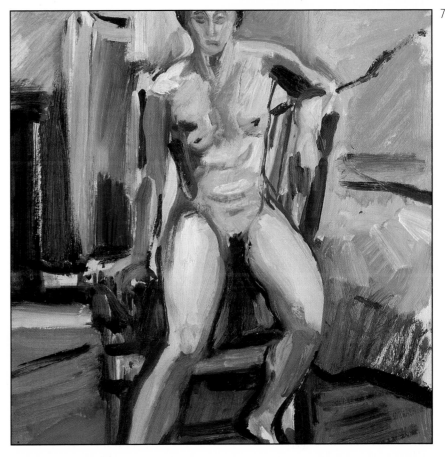

WOMAN BY A WINDOW

KAY GALLWEY

A change of medium to watercolor does not mean a change of approach. The thinking is the same. Watercolor is an ideal medium for seeing things broadly and simply. In exploiting the immediate and direct qualities of the medium, detail is subordinated to a feeling for the whole.

The artist is using a restricted palette of French ultramarine, permanent green, Vandyck brown, cadmium yellow, and cadmium red. The paper is a warm buff color, and the artist is using a no. 2 brush and small pieces of tissue.

1 A thin wash of light orange (mixed from cadmium red and yellow) is laid down for the figure, and a stronger cadmium red is used for the cloth against which the figure is standing. Some strokes of ultramarine into the wet paint surface give the slightest suggestion of form. The forms are softened with a tissue. A tissue can also be used to remove excess moisture.

2 One or two marks in Vandyck brown are placed to define the edges of the form.

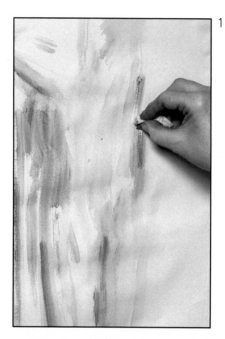
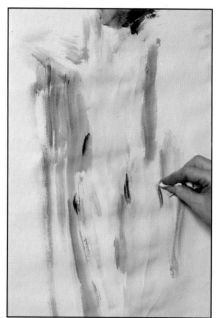

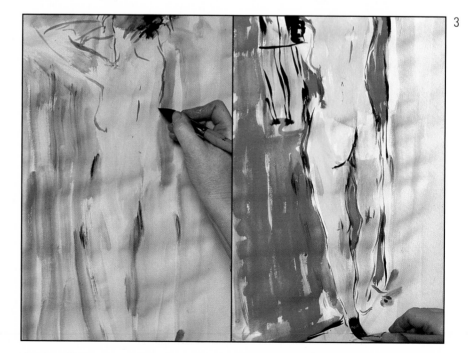

3 It is only at this stage that the artist begins to draw the form with any definition, using line. Prior to this she was only concerned with the main masses of the composition. Both ultramarine and brown are used in the drawing.

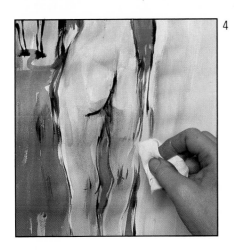
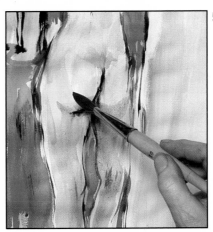
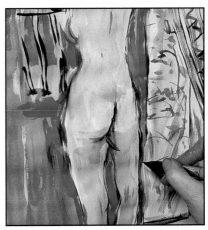

4 Using tissue, the artist is able to control the amount of bleeding and achieve just the right softness of line she requires.

5 The light washes of blue on the legs define the shadow well, and throw up the hips and buttocks into the light.

6 Right at the end of the painting the artist introduces pattern into the drapery and carpet, and into the foliage outside.

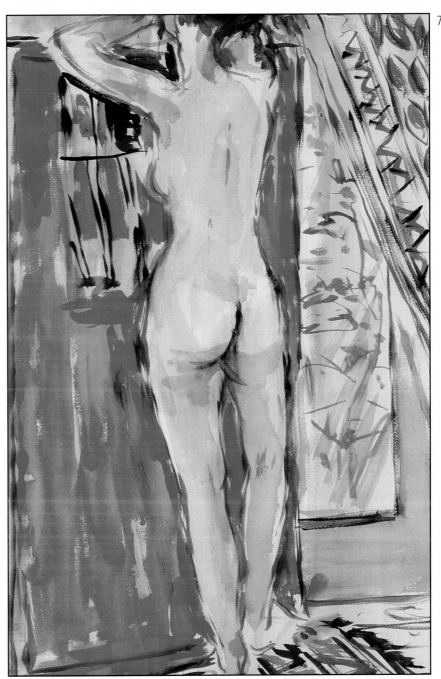

7 The final picture, which is the result of less than 30 minutes work, is a simple, satisfactory statement about the figure and its relationship to the room.

3

COMPOSING A PICTURE

Thinking about things simply, attempting to organize a jumble of appearances, and trying to make clear, simple statements inevitably introduce thoughts about composition. Decisions about the composition of a picture involve choices: what to keep and what to reject, whether to fill the picture space or to place the figure more deeply in space, whether to deal with part of the figure only and so on.

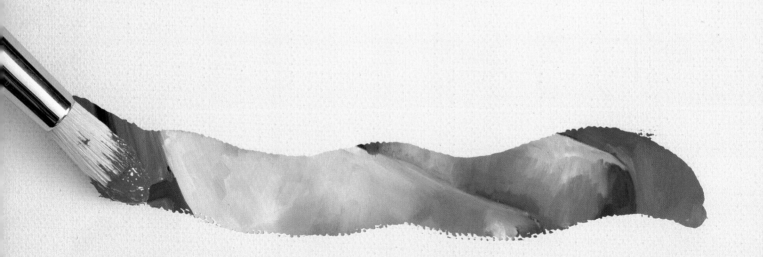

DARK-HAIRED WOMAN IN CHAIR

D A V I D   C A R R

This project is a study in oils which demonstrates the use of a space frame and the value of preparatory studies. These are an invaluable aid in composing a picture. However small, they help in making choices and in familiarizing oneself with the subject. It is important that the studies and the board or canvas on which the final picture is painted should have the same proportions. The process for matching the proportions of the painting board and those of the paper used for the preliminary studies is quite simple.

1 The model is in position and the artist has prepared his palette of French ultramarine, cobalt blue, viridian green, cadmium lemon, cadmium yellow, cadmium red, alizarin crimson, and titanium white. The brushes were no. 5 and no. 8 filbert, and no. 3 round hog-hair. It was painted on board prepared with a commercial white ground.

2 A space frame is a useful compositional device. It may be adequate to cut a rectangle out of the middle of a piece of card and hold it up to the subject, but this restricts the shape of the picture. A more flexible device can be made with two L-shaped pieces of card, which can be moved against each other to form a rectangle of varying proportions.

3 In this case the board was slightly smaller than the large piece of paper, and the artist has placed the board against the paper and drawn a line along the bottom. He then draws in the diagonals on the paper. Any two lines drawn from two neighboring sides, and at right-angles to them, that meet on the diagonal form a smaller rectangle that has exactly the same proportions as the larger one. (If the canvas is very large, a piece of paper is placed on the corner of the canvas and, using a long stick, the diagonal of the canvas is drawn across the paper.) The board is also shown squared up for the subsequent enlargement of a small study.

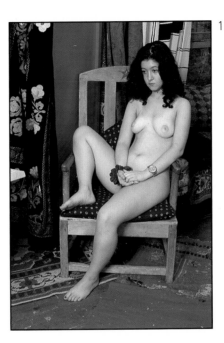

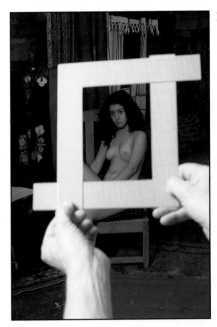

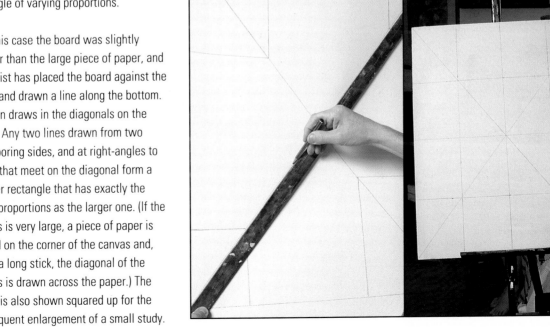

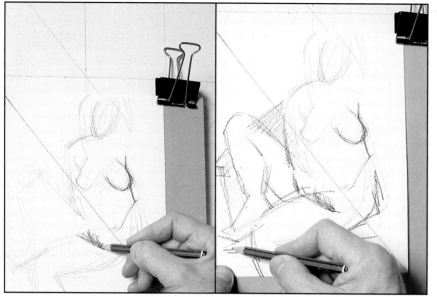

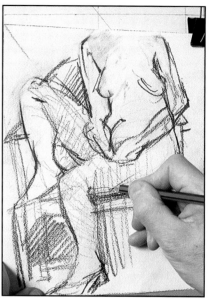

4 Having cut out one of the small paper rectangles which now has the same proportions as the board, the artist begins to make a simple drawing of the figure.

Having used the L-shaped pieces of card, he decides to let the figure fill the space, and he is making the study accordingly.

5 He makes a further study and manages to lose the head. Consequently he rejects this and decides he will probably use the first drawing.

6 He now squares up the small drawing using the same number of squares as on the larger board, and begins to transfer the drawing very simply using charcoal.

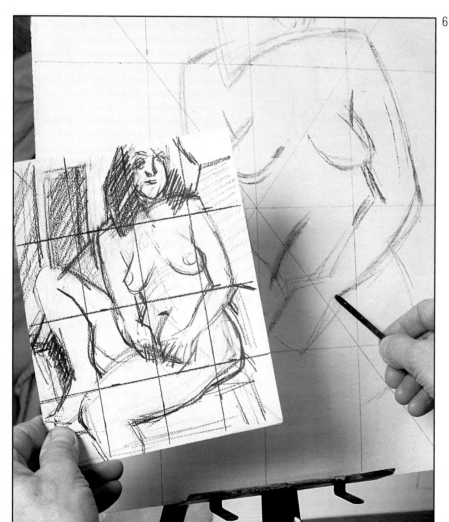
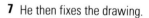

7 He then fixes the drawing.

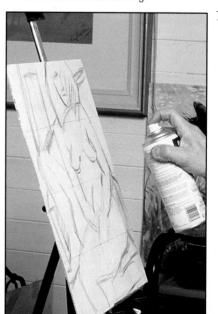

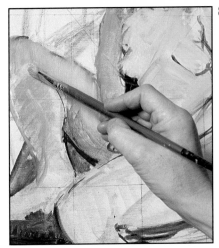

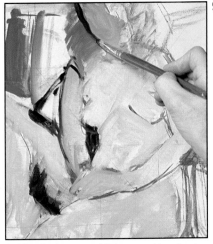

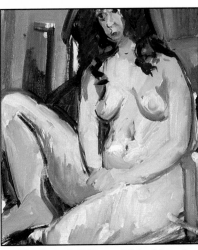

8 Looking at the model again, he begins to paint the flesh tones using a mixture of cadmium red and yellow. He draws the chair cushion in ultramarine, and defines some of the form using the same color.

9 His aim is to establish everything firmly and simply. He works color into the flesh and paints strong defining lines into the form. The shapes around the figure are developed.

10 The figure is fully established, but sits rather squarely in the chair. The flesh has been painted simply with basic yellows and pinks. The artist now works into this with neutral colors based on blue and green and redraws the figure.

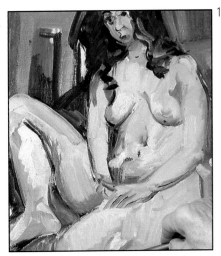

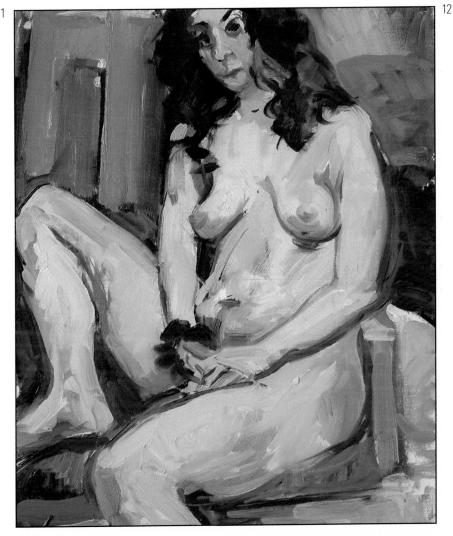

11 Gray/blue is worked into the stomach and under the model's right thigh, and slabs of paint push this leg back diagonally toward the chair back. The hair and face are defined more fully.

12 The point of this whole exercise is to make sure that the artist is in charge of the painting process right from the beginning to the end.

PRELIMINARY STUDIES

The importance of making preliminary studies cannot be overstressed. Time and effort spent thinking things out at this stage saves much frustration later on. Painting oneself into trouble takes seconds; painting oneself out of it can take hours.

RIGHT The artist, Jill Mumford, used a sketchbook to make a small gouache color study before starting her painting of the back of a seated nude. She decided to place the figure high on the page, and to make something of the large space in the foreground; it occupies almost half the picture. A clear, simple statement has established a composition with due regard for the distribution of shapes around the seated figure.

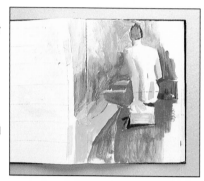

BELOW In the finished picture, done in oils, we feel that we are very close to the figure. The head has been cropped, and the foot just squeezes into the picture space. The artist has extended the dark tone of the thigh down the whole leg, and exploited the slabs of light falling on the back, floor and bed and the silhouette of the leg, thigh and breast.

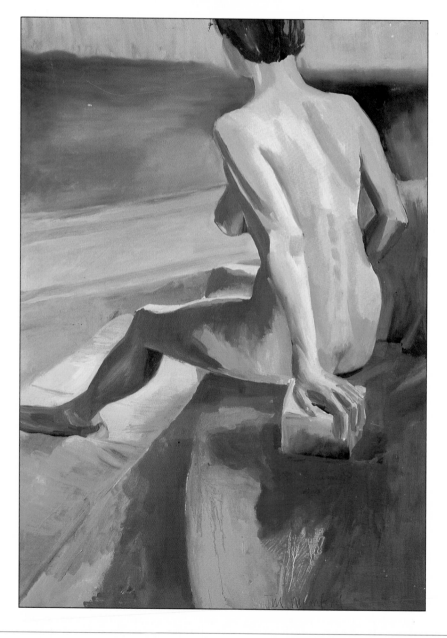

For the figure seated in the chair, Jill Mumford worked out the relationship of the figure to the floor, wall and chair in broad terms. The composition was worked out in more or less primary colors in oils, and the forms were seen in simplified terms.

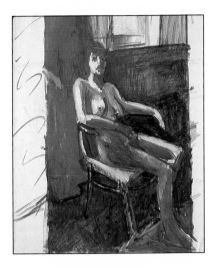

BELOW In the finished picture, in oils, the flesh tones and colors are more subtly modulated from warm to cool. The figure sits satisfactorily in the chair. The dramatic light on the figure clearly comes from a second window to the left, out of the picture.

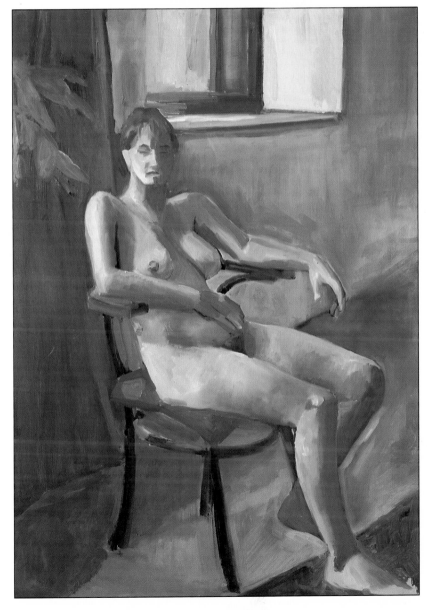

4
ALLA PRIMA TECHNIQUE

The commonest and most basic oil technique in use today is known as *alla prima*, meaning literally "at the first." The paint is applied in a direct and spontaneous manner, and it really came into its own in the 19th century. Instead of building up the paint stage by stage with successive layers of drawing, glazes (thin layers of transparent paint) and scumbles (layers of opaque paint dragged over existing layers of dry paint), the artist lays down each patch of color more or less as it is intended to appear finally.

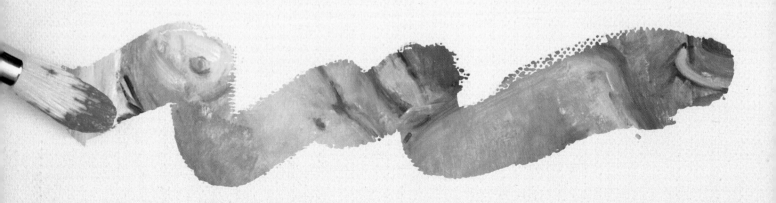

ALLA PRIMA IN OILS

The invention of the tin paint-tube in the 19th century helped artists to take the paints to the subject and paint it at one sitting. A painter like Van Gogh (1853–90) worked directly onto the canvas with a fully loaded brush, and the evidence is there in the clearly defined brushstrokes.

It is, however, possible to work wet into wet; that is, to apply paint over or into wet paint on the canvas, and at the same time build up a painting over a short space of time. The golden rule is to work "lean to fat." Any oil painting technique must obey this principle, otherwise the painting will crack and flake when it dries. Each successive layer of paint must have a little more oil in it. Dilution of the paint with turps at the beginning is a sound technique for initial drawing and early paint layers, but the full tube-paint consistency, with a little linseed oil added, should be used for subsequent layers.

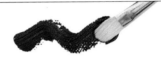

RECLINING WOMAN 1

JOY STEWART

This small *alla prima* oil study was painted in less than an hour. The artist used a restricted palette of yellow ocher, cadmium red light, alizarin crimson, French ultramarine, and titanium white. She is working on board primed with white acrylic, using no. 5 and no. 8 filbert hog-hair brushes.

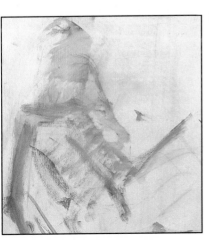

1 The model in a reclining position as seen by the artist.

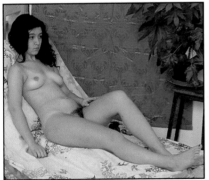

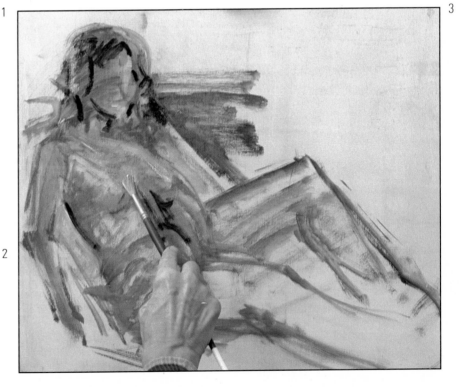

2 Without any preliminary charcoal drawing, the artist lays in the figure in terms of mass using a mixture of yellow ocher and cadmium red.

3 She begins to draw into this with alizarin crimson and French ultramarine.

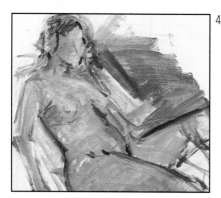

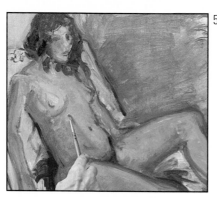

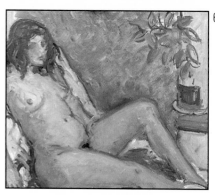

4 The wall is established, and boundary lines and points around the form hold the figure in place.

5 Using white, the artist begins to give the form more volume and to work some blue into the ocher flesh paint to define the darker parts of the form.

6 Using the same palette, the artist works into the fabric on the wall and the bed. The plant pot and the plant are painted in simply, introducing an additional lemon yellow mixed with ultramarine.

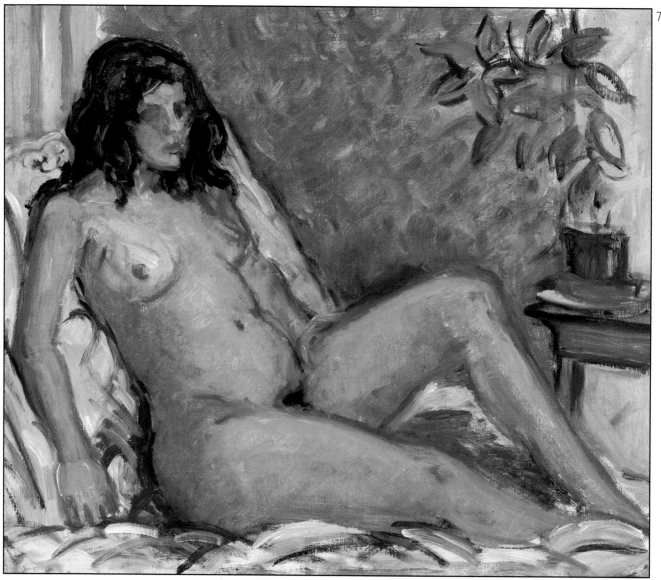

7 The volume of the figure is strengthened as the artist works wet into wet with light ocher, pinks from the alizarin, and purples from mixing ultramarine and alizarin.

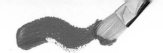

RECLINING WOMAN 2

S U S A N   C A R T E R

This oil painting of the same pose from a different angle illustrates the principle of working from lean to fat. The artist is using much the same palette as in the preceding project, with an additional light red, viridian green, burnt umber, and a mineral violet. She likes to use a painting medium made from about two-thirds turps to one-third oil.

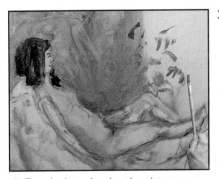

1 The model in pose.

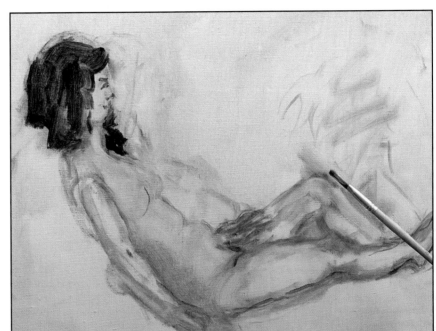

2 The initial drawing has been done with paint thinned with plenty of medium. The artist soon sets about laying down thin masses of color over the whole canvas.

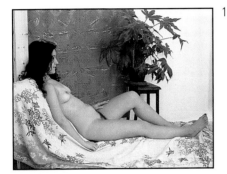

3 The aim is to develop the picture as a whole.

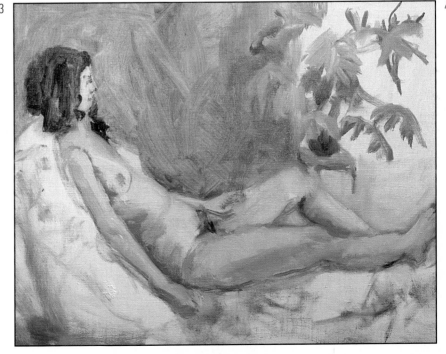

4 The artist paints the flesh using light red, yellow ocher and white, and draws into it using blues and umber.

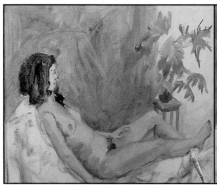 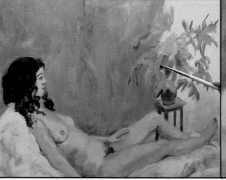

5 It is important to keep moving around the canvas, adjusting each part to preserve a credible sense of light throughout.

Touches of warmth are introduced into the cloth. The result is a light and airy study.

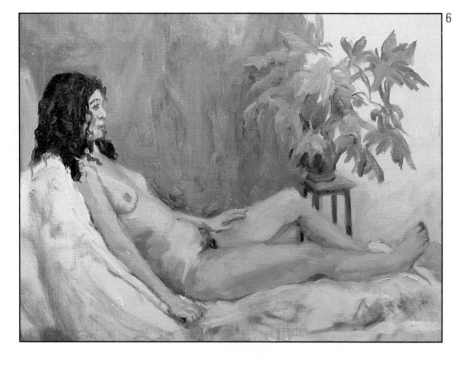

6

6 By continual attention to the whole picture surface, the artist has attained a sense of completeness rather than finish.

RAPID *ALLA PRIMA* STUDY

This small study of the reclining nude against a tartan rug was completed in around an hour, and is another example of the use of the *alla prima* technique with oils.

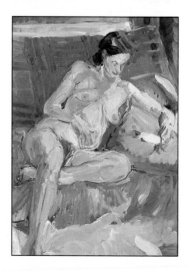

LEFT A standard palette of French ultramarine, cobalt blue, viridian green, cadmium lemon, cadmium yellow, cadmium red, alizarin crimson, and titanium white was used. A small amount of turps has been used to help the paint flow a little. It is painted on board on a white ground. Plenty of warm yellows and light oranges have been used for the light flesh, in contrast with the cooler blues and pinks in the shadows. The brushstrokes follow the direction of the forms.

ALLA PRIMA IN WATERCOLOR

The term *alla prima* is never used in watercolor, as in a sense watercolor is always *alla prima*. It is an immediate medium that does not improve with overworking. Confidence and a sure touch, which can only come from practice, are needed.

A very useful way to train the eye and hand, and to experiment with watercolor at the same time, is to take numerous small pieces of paper cut or torn from a larger sheet and force yourself to work rapidly and simply.

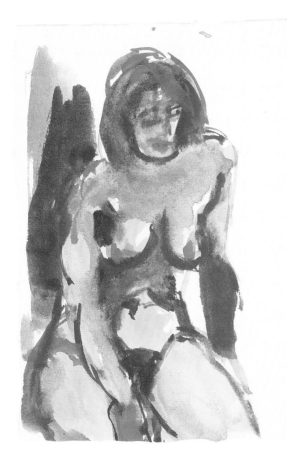

LEFT AND BELOW These small watercolor studies by David Carr probably took less than 10 minutes. First a light wash of warm color was laid down, with the side of the brush following the main direction of the torso, head and limbs. While the paint was still damp, and using drier paint and the point of the brush, ultramarine and crimson mixed was drawn into this. Thin washes of cooler paint were glazed over the warm areas where the figure is in shadow, giving a sense of form and movement.

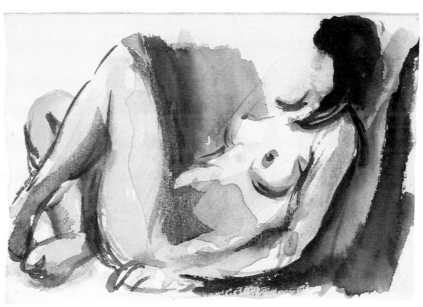

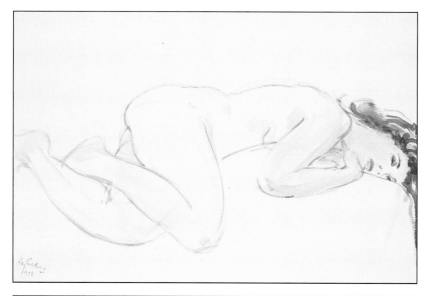

LINEAR WATERCOLOR SKETCHES

These linear watercolor studies show how effective this technique can be in describing the volume and fluidity of the human body. The ability to work quickly is all-important in achieving this effect.

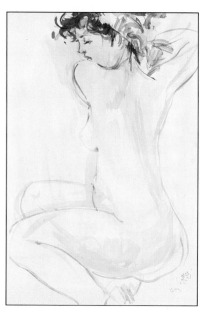

ABOVE AND LEFT This artist, Kay Gallwey, has taken a more linear approach in her simple watercolor studies of the nude. The stronger lines were added last. She began by taking very watery pinks and light ochers, and followed the main direction of the form, the curve of the spine being crucial. The volume of the thigh was felt, and then the langorous line of light umber lapped around the form already suggested. The final marks gave the details of headscarf and hair. She employs the same technique in other work. It is essential to work quickly, and constant practice is necessary to gain this amount of fluidity.

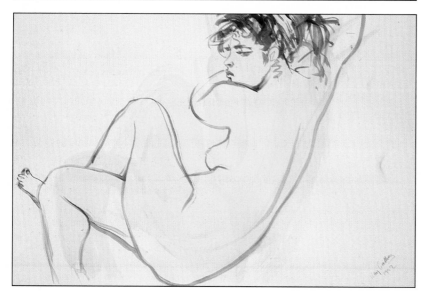

ALLA PRIMA IN OILS USING THICKER PAINT

These three paintings demonstrate the variety of rich and powerful effects that can result from the use of thick paint applied with brushes, palette knives, and even with the fingers.

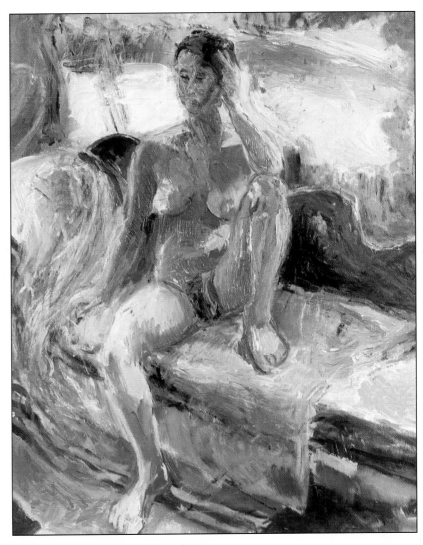

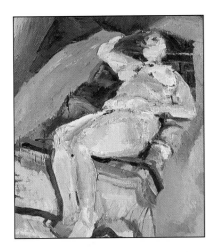

ABOVE Thick oil paint has been used in the study of the reclining nude on the striped bedspread. The problem was to maintain consistent light on the figure and the fabric. White was mixed with most of the colors, but not to the extent of making them chalky. The passage down the form moves from warm to cool continuously. The orange of the arm contrasts with the blue-greens of the torso, and cool pinks play against warmer yellows. Thick oil paint and a palette knife were used throughout.

RIGHT Here the artist, Mike Knowles, has used large brushes, palette knives and tins of oil paint. The continuous working and reworking of the painting by scraping off and restating the forms has built up an encrusted paint surface. Slabs of paint and strong drawing make a powerful final statement, the result of prolonged observation.

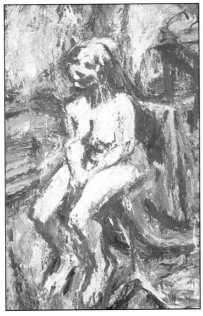

ABOVE Some time was spent drawing the figure quite carefully, but once the main forms were established, thick paint was applied very freely. The objective was to describe the figure against the light without loosing the warmth, and raw sienna and alizarin crimson tempered with French ultramarine were used to paint these darker masses. The complementary contrasts have been exploited – the blues behind the figure against the orange blanket cascading onto the floor, the lilacs against the splashes of yellow on the windows and the chaise-longue. Not only were large brushes used here, but the artist's fingers were dipped in the paint, drawing directly to keep the paint fresh and sparkling. It is said that Titian in later life used his fingers to work in the richer areas of his paintings.

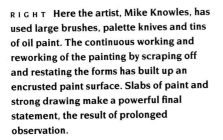

SEEING PLANES AND STRUCTURE

The fundamental problem facing the painter is that of dealing with a three-dimensional world of space and volume, and of translating that onto a two-dimensional surface. One of the most important steps is to look for planes. A plane is a way of expressing the changes of direction that occur across a form. Outline as such does not exist, and a contour is merely the point at which a plane turns out of sight. It is light that gives the clue to form, and as a form turns we can see the shadow edge, which from another viewpoint would be a contour. This shadow edge is a change of plane.

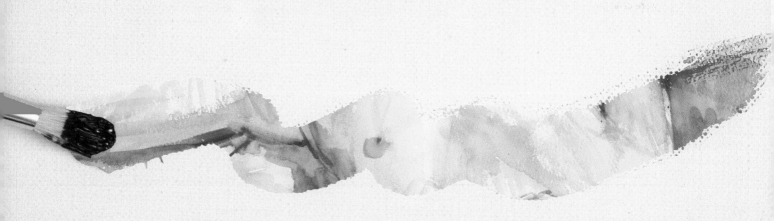

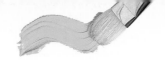

GIRL LYING ON RUGS

DAVID CARR

In this watercolor the artist is building up a series of planes with thin directional strokes of color. This is painted using a glaze technique (pages 104–11) as well as some wet-into-wet (see pages 112–16) on 140 lb (300 gsm) – "not" surface paper. The palette consists of French ultramarine, cerulean blue, cobalt green light, cadmium lemon, cadmium yellow, cadmium red, alizarin crimson, and ultramarine violet.

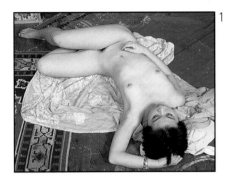

1 The model was positioned on the floor with the artist standing looking down on the figure.

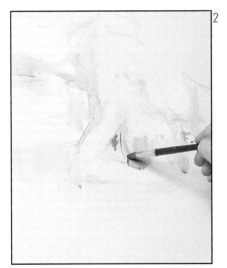

2 The first marks begin to deal with the large triangular plane of the upper chest. The palest dilute alizarin, cadmium red, and cerulean blue have been used here.

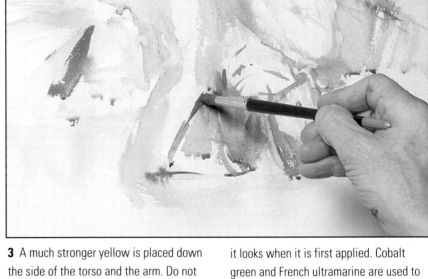

3 A much stronger yellow is placed down the side of the torso and the arm. Do not be afraid of watercolor. It dries paler than it looks when it is first applied. Cobalt green and French ultramarine are used to begin defining the floor.

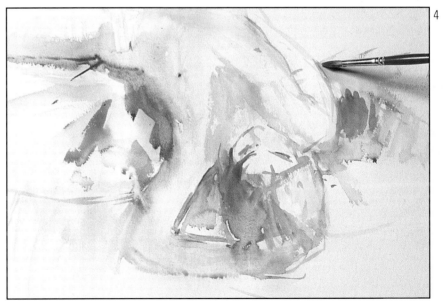

4 The floor is developed, and a dilute cadmium red is used to establish the side plane of the thighs. Some linear work under the thigh and around the hip defines what was first described by planes.

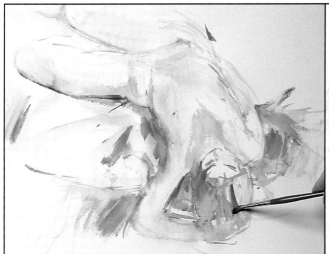 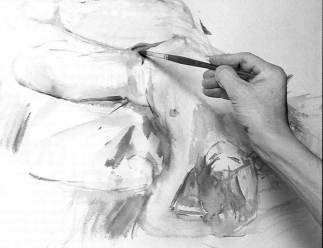

5 Marks follow the direction of the planes felt in the floor. Greater volume is given to the head and body. The planes on the top of the thighs are drawn with line. The painting has been conceived in terms of planes. In other words, the planes were found first so that the position of the contours could be located.

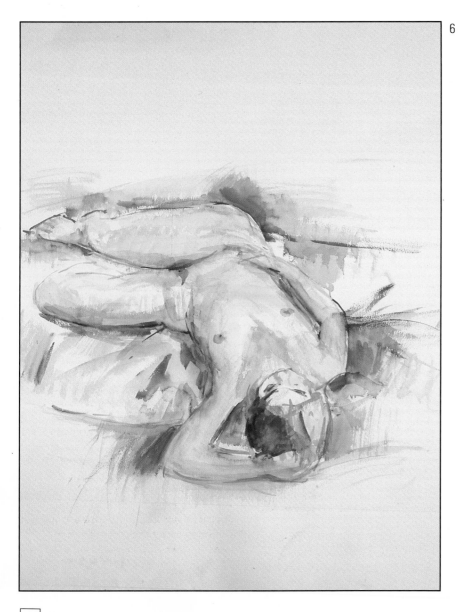
6

6 The light and transparent marks follow the direction of the planes, and the white of the paper has been used as a positive element.

ESTABLISHING CLEAR STRUCTURAL PLANES

These paintings all show the artists' awareness of strong directional light producing clearly defined planes.

The artist, Sharon Finmark, has glazed plane upon plane in her watercolor of a reclining nude on a settee. She has used color mainly for the darker tones; for some of the lighter tones she has left the paper white. She used a restricted palette of French ultramarine, cadmium yellow, cadmium red, and alizarin crimson.

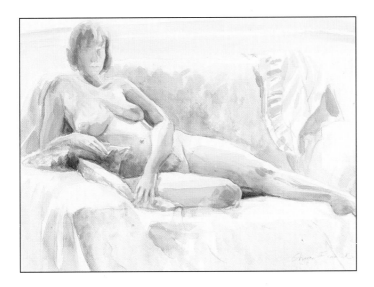

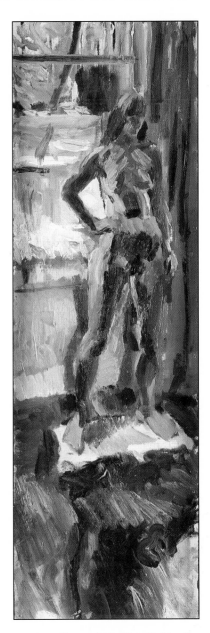

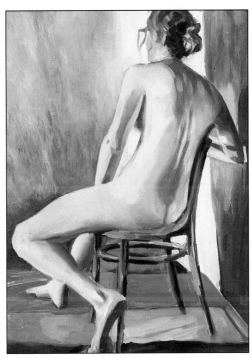

The marks in this tall, thin oil painting follow the direction of each form. Although the figure stood against the light and the bent arm was in silhouette, there was a high light-source from a lightbulb in the room. The figure's weight was thrown forward at the hips, pushing the legs into shadow. There was an almost step-like change of plane at the stomach. Painted over a warm sienna base for the figure, the lighter planes were put in using yellow ocher with touches of blue and yellow. The darker planes were described by strong directional strokes of viridian green, and deep purples and blue-grays using a mixture of ultramarine and alizarin crimson.

The gradation of planes up the back and shoulders is well felt in this oil painting by Jill Mumford. Over a predominantly warm skin tone, the violet and deep crimson planes move up from the base of the spine and follow the curving form of the shoulders. The lighter areas were seen in warm and cold yellows. Note the structural work of the left arm, the shadows cast on the inside of the right arm, and the sharply defined planes of the calf and foot.

USING BRUSHMARKS TO FOLLOW THE FORM

The pair of oil studies below, by David Carr, show the same pose under different light conditions. As all four of these paintings demonstrate, whether the picture is a full figure in a complex space or a more intimate portrait, an awareness of planes is important.

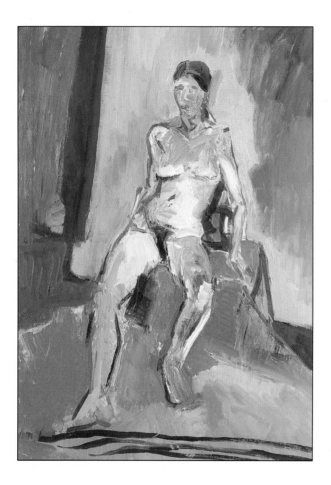

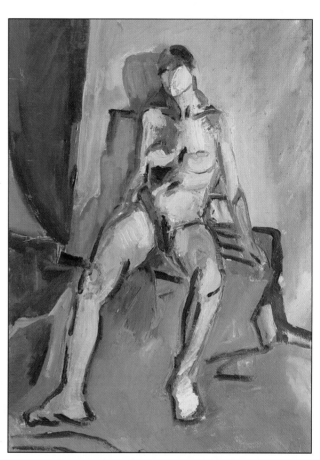

A B O V E In the lighter of the two, the planes were knocked in rapidly, using multi-directional strokes. A slab of orange described the upper chest, and then lighter ocher followed the planes of the stomach and pelvis, and the inside thigh of the extended leg. The structure was brought together by strong lines of blue-black, which cut into the form to emphasize the direction of the planes.

A B O V E The darker picture was painted under artificial light, hence the harsh tonal jumps and the clear shadow cast by the figure. The lighter parts of the flesh were painted using yellow ocher, cadmium red and white mixed, and the darker masses with green and blue-grays. Again, strong lines pulled the form together at the end.

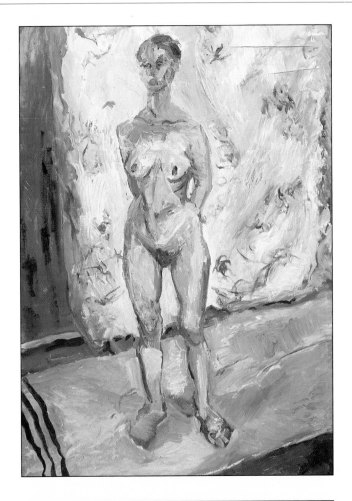

LEFT This is a large oil painting (5 × 4 ft/ 1.5 × 1.2 m) by David Carr taken to a greater degree of finish than the seated studies. Painted very much in an *alla prima* technique, the palette was cadmium yellow pale, cadmium yellow mid, yellow ocher, cadmium red, alizarin crimson, French ultramarine, and titanium white. The final drawing of the figure was done in thick, dark lines, over which the directional brushmarks followed the planes. Light blues and violets were used to describe the darker form, which was generally high-keyed. Around the cheek and neck, this cooler color is sharply contrasted with the highlight on the cheekbone. Strong, light pink ochers (yellow ocher, cadmium red, and white) start above the breasts and follow the form of the stomach, thighs, and shins. Note the slab of paint travelling across the right shin below the knee. The artist was standing while painting this, and felt the importance of establishing the feet firmly and giving the feeling of looking down onto the top of a plane.

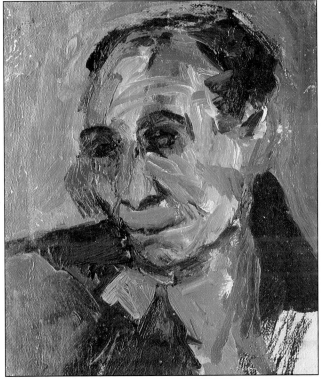

LEFT The artist, David Carr, was very aware of the way the planes flowed around the head in this small oil study of a friend. Again done *alla prima*, a warmer initial layer of paint comprising cadmium red and yellow ocher was worked into, using directional strokes of light yellow ocher. The brush moved around the forehead, almost skipping over the color beneath. The plane of the side of the face and cheek was strongly established, and a few strokes of light blue bring around the jaw.

ANATOMY

The preceding sections have been concerned with thinking in painterly terms, with seeing things simply and being selective in making decisions about composition. After the problems of representing a three-dimensional world on a flat surface have been considered, the figure itself needs to be looked at in greater depth. Confidence in painting the figure comes from knowing something of the "vocabulary" of the figure – its anatomy. A great depth of anatomical knowledge is not essential – only that known as "superficial anatomy," which concerns itself with the way certain bones, muscles and tendons affect the surface form, needs to be understood.

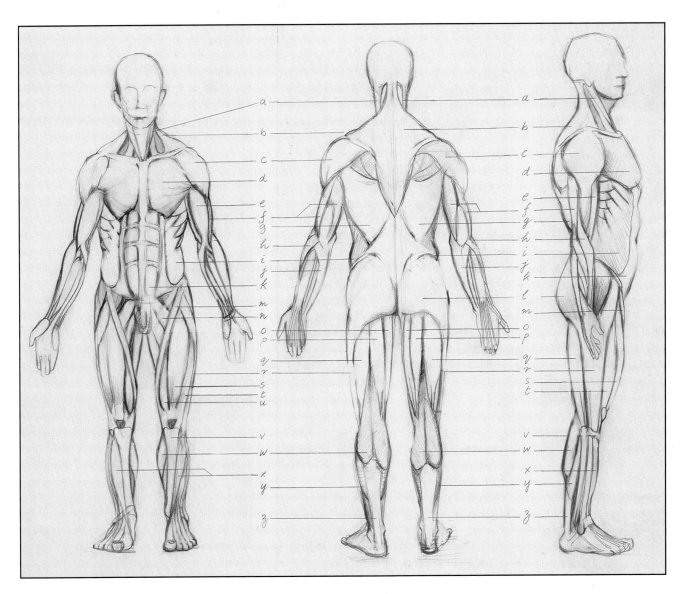

ABOVE **These three drawings of the figure from different positions show all the main muscles of the body.**

Here is an ABC of the figure – 26 important points to help in a confident and authoritative approach. The standing figure shows off the muscles to good advantage. Whatever position the figure takes, these same muscles can be found, either tensed or at rest.

The somewhat complex names of some muscles make sense when analysed. Frequently they describe the progress of the muscle. The *sterno-mastoid* (a) travels from the sternum (breastbone) to the mastoid process behind the ear. The *rectus femoris* (r) originates in the rectal area and attaches to the end of the femur (thighbone).

Around the head, neck, and shoulders the main muscles are the *sterno-mastoid* (a) and the almost diamond- or trapezoid-shaped *trapezius* (b). The *trapezius* begins at the base of the skull, travels far down the back, attaches itself to the shoulder blades at the side, and continues over the shoulders to connect with the collarbone (clavicle) at the front. It is this muscle that gives the characteristic slope to the shoulders. This is dealt with in greater depth on page 54.

The *latissimus dorsi* (g) – there is one on each side of the back – laps around the ribs and tucks up underneath the armpits, attaching to the upper armbone (humerus) at the top. At the front, the large *pectoral muscles* (d) move from the breastbone (sternum) up to the collarbones, and out to the upper ends of the arms. The long, flat muscle down the front of the body is known as the *rectus abdominis* (k) and is divided into four main parts, which are more or less clearly seen depending on the muscularity of the person. The *external obliques* (i) move out from the *rectus abdominis*, around the waist area, and up to the *latissimus dorsi*.

The shape of the shoulders is completed by the *deltoid* (c). Viewed from the side, it is like an inverted triangle (the sign for *delta* in the Greek alphabet is a triangle). It covers the arm joint rather like a raglan sleeve in shape. It moves down the arm and tucks in between the *biceps* (e) and the *triceps* (f).

Much of the characteristic shape of the outside of the lower arm or forearm is created by the *supinator longus* (h) – *supinate* means to turn – together with the long *radial extensor* of the wrist immediately below it. On the inner side are the group of muscles that move the fingers and cause the inner bulge. The outermost of these is the *ulnar flexor* (j) of the wrist, seen most clearly from the back.

At the front of the legs the *sartorius* (m), a long, thin muscle, travels from the pelvis, in and across the leg, down to the top of the lower leg and attaches to the tibia (main lower-leg or shinbone). It is essential to look for this muscle in defining the leg. The three large muscles – the *rectus femoris* (s), the *outer vastus* (t), and *inner vastus* (u) – although clearly defined, especially when tensed, are really part of one large muscle, which has a common tendon

connecting it to the kneecap (patella). On the inner side of the thigh, moving into the pubic area, is a group of muscles known as *adductors* (n).

At the back, the *gluteus maximus* (l) and the *gluteus medius* form the buttocks. It is important to note how these muscles are attached by a strong tendon to the *ilio-tibial band* (r), which flattens the outside of the thigh and travels right down to the top of the *tibia* (v).

The back of the thigh is composed of the three long flexor muscles of the knee – the *biceps* (q) and the grandly named *semi-membranosus* (o) and *semi-tendinous* (p). They originate from the pelvis and are covered at the top by the buttocks. They produce the fullness of the back of the thigh. When the knee is bent they stand out as prominent chords, and they are often referred to as the hamstrings.

The most pronounced muscle down the front of the lower leg, just at the side of the shin, is the *tibialis anticus* (x), and at the back the calf is made up of two main muscles. The underlying and flatter one, not unlike a flat fish in form, is aptly called the *soleus* (y), while the predominant muscle is called the *gastrocnemius* (Latin for the belly of a toad). It has two heads, the inside one being lower than the outer. Last, but not least, as it is the largest tendon in the body, the *Achilles tendon* (z) connects the *soleus* and *gastrocnemius* to the heel.

Of necessity, these are anatomical diagrams and are idealized in form, but it is an important practice to draw from anatomy books. Often, well-illustrated medical books are extremely useful. Above all, an understanding of the mechanics of the human body is crucial.

CONTRAPPOSTO

From classical times a standing pose known as *contrapposto* has been one of the archetypes that have appeared and reappeared. It is an ideal state of equilibrium created by contrary movements of the body. Whatever position the figure takes, there is a push and pull of opposing forces enabling it to stand. *Contrapposto* illustrates well how these forces and balances operate.

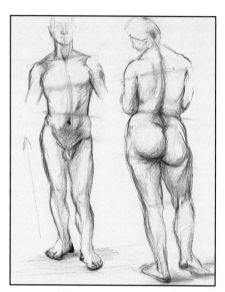

A B O V E **When looking at a standing figure, it is important to note which leg is bearing the weight – it is seldom equally distributed except on a parade-ground. Here, one leg clearly carries the weight, and there is a pronounced change of plane at the great trochanter, which is the bony protuberance at the top of the thigh (from the femur or thighbone). There is a clear diagonal axis across the top of the pelvis. This becomes slightly less pronounced at the waist. The spine curves away, dropping the shoulder above the weight-bearing leg. The diagonal axis therefore changes dramatically at the pectoral muscles and shoulder blades, and the shoulders balance the opposing movement of the pelvis.**

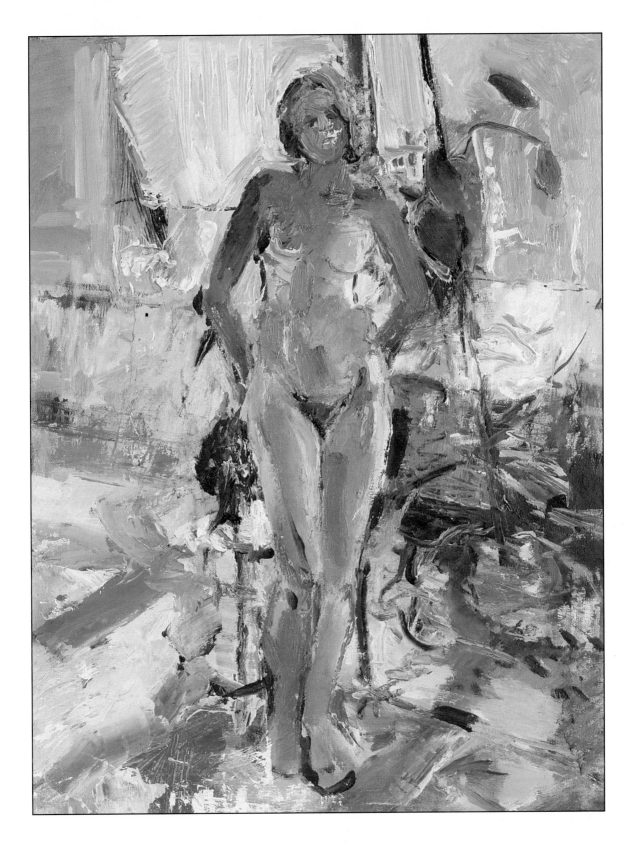

ABOVE This standing nude, painted in oils by the author, involved the *contrapposto* pose quite unconsciously on the part of the model. It also happens to be *contro luce* or *contre jour* – against the light. She was leaning against a chair with her arms behind her back. Her left leg is clearly carrying the weight, as the right leg is bent. Notice the axes of the pelvis, the waist, breasts and shoulders moving in opposite directions. It is broadly painted, and much of the room is done with a palette knife and impasto (paint applied very thickly). A great deal of white was used in the space to give a shimmer of light. The base color of the figure is raw sienna into which slabs of indigo, alizarin crimson, and cadmium red follow the direction of the planes.

BALANCE AND WEIGHT

This series of small watercolors by David Carr explores the problem of balancing the figure and describing the forces at work. Each painting is done from a slightly different angle.

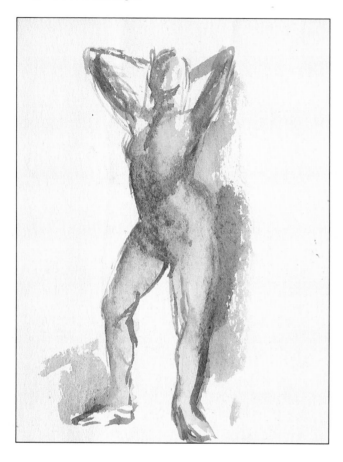

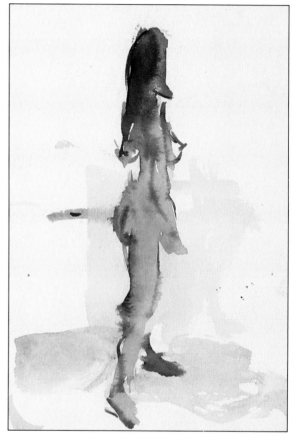

ABOVE In this standing nude with the arms raised above the head, the weight is on the left leg, and the enormous change of direction at the waist bears this out. Looking carefully at the watercolor, you will see that the mass of the figure was first established with a warm yellow (aureolin), and the drawing with French ultramarine into the damp paint followed. A brush loaded with ultramarine was taken up the torso with just a touch of alizarin crimson. Three primaries have been used to express the "idea" of standing.

ABOVE In this little watercolor, the figure turns and takes the weight off the right leg, transferring it to the left. Again painted with minimal means, a dark violet (French ultramarine and alizarin crimson) was drawn into a warmer wash. Note the slight bleeding of the color, which helps to give a sense of form.

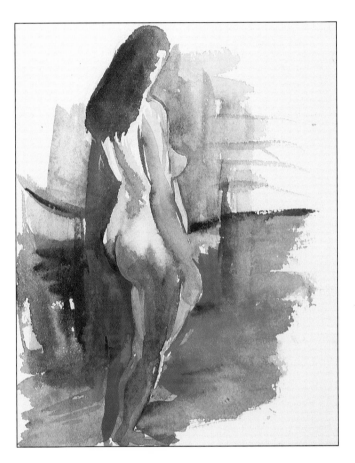

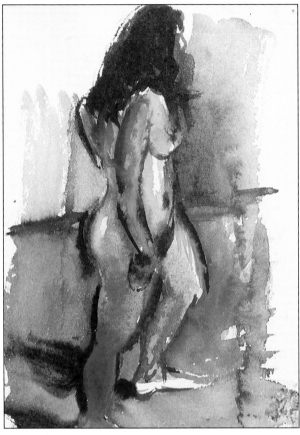

ABOVE In this, more of the back was visible. A pale, flat yellow established the shape of the figure. A strong red line was placed down the leg carrying the weight, over which a glaze of French ultramarine put the whole leg in shadow, creating a powerful change of plane at the hip.

ABOVE Here, the artist moved around to the front to see more of the stomach and the bent leg. Again, cadmium red was worked into aureolin. Extremely dense lines were painted into that with a mixture of French ultramarine and cadmium red, which gives almost black. This is most noticeable in the hair, but it also helps to give tension to the weight-bearing leg. The cast shadow from the legs helps to give a sense of direction to the plane of the floor.

7

HEAD, NECK, AND SHOULDERS

When you come to paint the head and shoulders, it is of the utmost importance to understand the basic structure of this area. Here is a brilliant piece of engineering, allowing the head to rock backwards and forwards on the first vertebra (the atlas), while turning from side to side on the second (the axis).

So often the head is conceived as if it were a football stuck on top of a pole, when a rudimentary knowledge of this crucial area would inform and articulate the painting so much more.

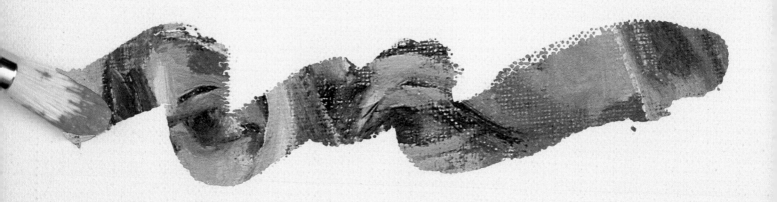

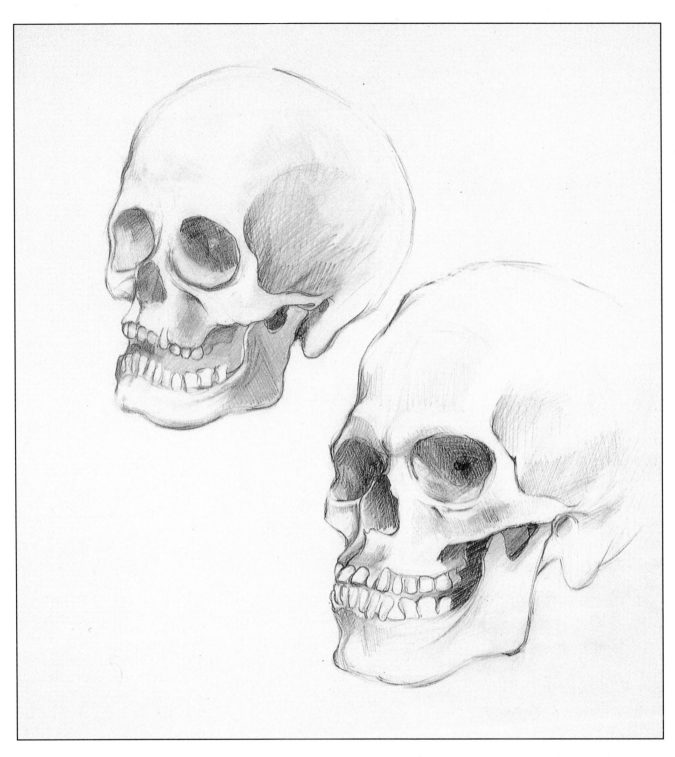

Looking at the skull, you can see the differences between the male and the female. The male tends to be a little squarer, and the brow is more prominent. The male forehead tends to slope backwards, whereas the female is more vertical. The jawbone is larger in the male. The angle at the back of the female jaw is much

ABOVE **These two drawings of the skull show the basic differences between the male and the female – the lower of the two is the male.**

gentler. Note the cheekbone (malar), which moves right up the side of the eye, and how it is joined to the side of the skull by a slender bone known as the zygomatic arch. The skull is made up of a series of bones fused immovably together, and the only moving bone is the lower jaw, or mandible.

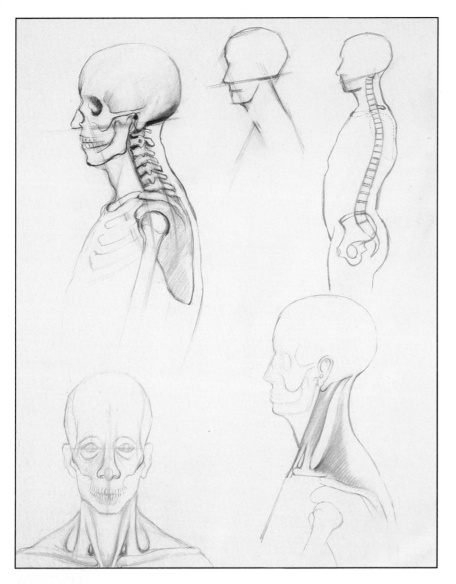

This illustrates three important points. First, the *back* of the skull is much *higher* than the base of the jawbone or chin. This may be obscured by the hair, in which case the base of the skull is often placed too low. Second, the spine does not enter the head vertically, but at an angle. It then proceeds to describe a shallow S from shoulder to waist to pelvis. And third – the most important point – the mastoid process, a lump (process) of bone, can be found immediately below and behind the ear. Even if the hair obscures it, you know where it is if you note the position of the ear, and this gives you the base of the skull.

From this point comes the sterno-mastoid muscle, so important in giving the neck its characteristic form. It starts at the mastoid process and then divides, one part being attached to the top of the sternum or breastbone, the other to the inner end of the clavicle or collarbone. The windpipe and throat move forward at an opposing angle from behind the breastbone, moving up between the sterno-mastoid muscles into the jaw.

The other main muscle involved is the trapezius, which travels from the back of the head down to the scapula or shoulder blade, forming the ridge that gives the shoulder its slope. Note how the sterno-mastoid and the trapezius tense and relax as the head moves from side to side. If you look in a mirror and hunch your shoulders forward, note the pits that appear between the muscles and the collarbones.

ABOVE LEFT Drawing to show the relative positions of the skull, spine, and sterno-mastoid muscle.

LEFT Drawing that demonstrates the action of the sterno-mastoid muscle.

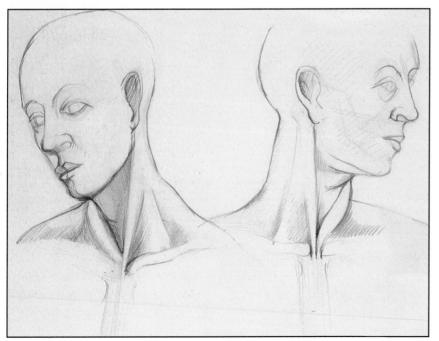

PORTRAIT HEAD

D A V I D   C A R R

W hen painting this portrait, the author took care over the points described earlier in this chapter.
It is important to feel the volume of the skull under the skin, and to see that the hair follows
this volume and is not added as if it is a wig. It is sometimes a good idea to ask a female sitter to put
her hair up so you can observe the base of the skull at the back more clearly.
The palette for this was French ultramarine, cobalt blue, cerulean blue, cobalt green, viridian green,
raw umber, cadmium lemon, cadmium yellow, yellow ocher, cadmium red, alizarin crimson,
and titanium white. The brushes used were no. 8 filbert, no. 3 round hog-hair and no. 8 sable-nylon mix.
It was painted on canvas primed with an egg tempera ground.

1 The model in position with the light
coming from the left.

2 The initial drawing was done very lightly
using a minimum amount of charcoal and
mainly with a very dilute mixture of raw
umber and ultramarine. The light was
coming from the left. The lighter parts of
the face, head, and shoulder were
established with a mixture of cadmium
yellow, cadmium red, and yellow ocher
plus white. Then ultramarine, raw umber,
and cadmium red were used to define the
darker parts. The artist was very aware of
the volume of the skull and its height at
the back beneath the hair. The sterno-
mastoid has been very clearly painted in,
as has the zygomatic arch leading from the
cheek to the ear.

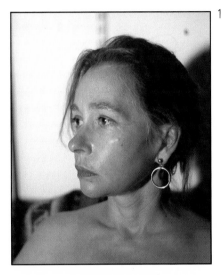

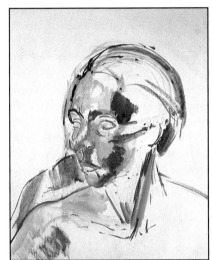

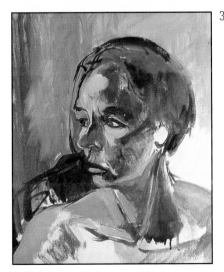

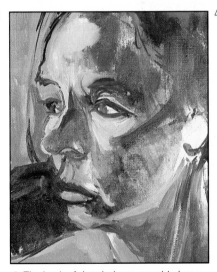

3 Cobalt blue and green, viridian green,
cadmium lemon, and alizarin crimson
were being used. To paint the wall behind
the figure, the artist used largely viridian
and cobalt blue with some white and
yellow ocher.

4 The back of the chair on one side has
been defined very strongly. These slabs of
color will be important in establishing the
profile. Note the continued attention to the
underlying form.

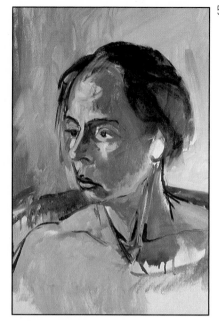

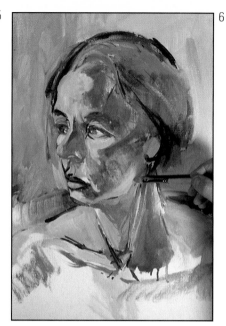

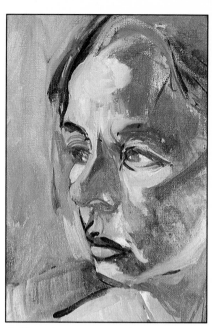

5 The trapezius muscle has now been established and therefore the shoulders, and the structure of the neck has been further clarified, showing that the throat comes out between the sterno-mastoid muscles. The hair should always follow the form of the skull.

6 The chair and wall have been further defined. The artist drew into the head with an ultramarine/raw umber mixture, constructing the eye more clearly and defining the hair traveling around the head.

7 The artist was aware of some reflected light from the body under the chin.

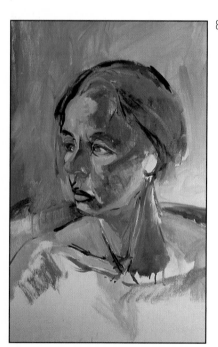

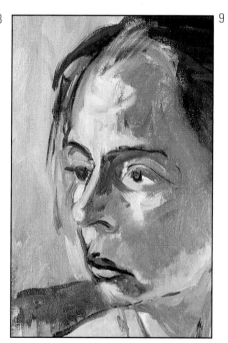

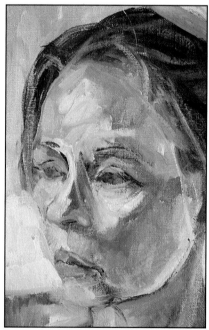

8 The artist noted a rhythm of shadow down the forehead, cheek and neck, and, in establishing this, flattened the face too much and lost some of its volume. Consequently the actual likeness has gone to an extent.

9 Note in the detail, however, that the planes around the eye and down the side of the nose have been developed. The forehead needs to be broader and the cheekbone should be redefined. The chin is also weak.

10 This reworking has been done using a light flesh tone of cadmium yellow and cadmium red with white and some yellow ocher. The way the hair flows around the head has been emphasized. The lips are fuller, as is the chin.

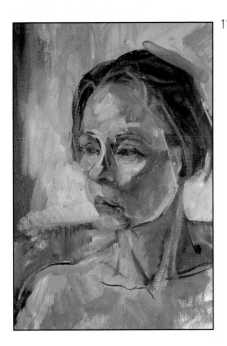 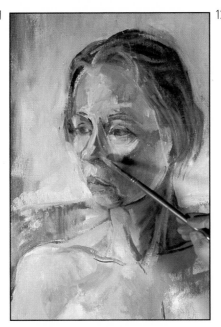 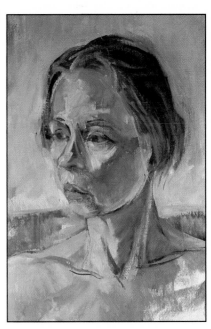

11

12

13

11 Adjustments have also been made to the head and neck, and the artist has built up the planes on the shoulders and upper chest using the same flesh tones, but modulated with a little ultramarine and alizarin crimson.

12 Some warmth has been introduced into the nostril to bring the nose around, and a light plane has been introduced just under the eye to bring the lower lid around the eyeball. It is important that eyelids follow the volume of the eyeball underneath. A light blue-gray has been used to establish the whites of the eyes. The use of pure white should be avoided as it is usually tonally too sharp.

13 Some violet in the wall behind the head and neck helps to give the flesh a sense of light by reacting with the yellow. The green (both the dark patch on the left and the light green-yellow under the violet) acts against the warmer areas of red in the figure.

14 The picture underwent several changes and at one point was almost lost. The successful conclusion shows the importance of constant reference to structure in rescuing form.

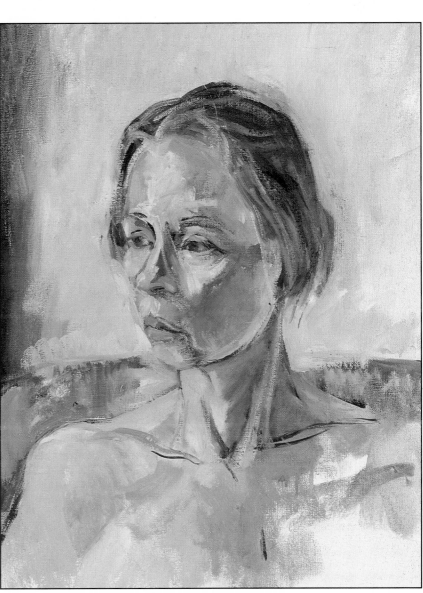

14

HEAD, NECK, AND SHOULDERS 57

8

THE FACE AND ITS FEATURES

W e should now look more closely at the head and, in particular, the face. There are quite a number of muscles involved in the many subtle facial expressions that people make. Do not be alarmed, however, as we only need to look at those muscles beneath the skin that give the face its characteristic form.

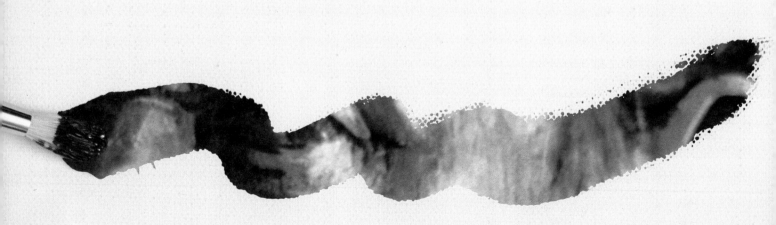

The whole of the skull is covered by a thin film of muscle. A muscle at the side of the skull – the *temporal muscle* (a) – travels down behind the *zygomatic arch* (b) onto the jawbone. This together with the *masseter* (g), that large muscle traveling from the cheekbone to the jaw, is involved in opening and closing the mouth. You will often see the masseter flexing when someone grits their teeth in determination.

Coming from the inside top of the nose, muscles travel down each side of the nose to the inside edges of the nostrils and the corners of the

upper lip. These are the *elevators* of the upper lip and nostrils (d). They raise the corners of the mouth and the nostrils and cause the characteristic furrow between the nose and the cheeks, especially pronounced in the male.

Other muscles move away from each corner of the mouth, notably the *buccinator* (f), which can pull the side of the mouth back and expel air between the teeth and the cheek. The *zygomaticus major* (e) and *minor* (c) similarly lift the corner of the mouth and upper lip, especially if the person is sneering.

The sling-like *depressors* (h) of the lower lip and angle of the mouth pull the jaw open and lower the corners of the mouth. It should be noted that a ring of muscle encircles the entire mouth, and it is with this that we close the mouth firmly and purse our lips. It is known as the *orbicularis oris*, and the surrounding muscles (buccinator, depressors, and elevators) interlace with it to enable us to move our mouth in any way we wish.

The eye is similarly surrounded by a circular muscle – the *orbicularis oculi*. This is involved in squinting and closing the eye. The most important point here is that the amount of the eye that we see is only a small proportion of its total size. It is spherical and slightly egg-shaped, and goes back deep into the skull. We should be most particular to note that the eyelids follow its spherical shape. Neither is the eye an almond shape pointed at each corner. The tear duct, not unlike a teardrop itself, occupies the corner near the nose. At the outer corner, the upper lid always crosses the lower lid.

The nose is about two-thirds gristle or cartilage (the shaded area), and it is only at the top that there is a bone (see the skull). If you are unfortunate enough to acquire a broken nose, it is this small bone that is broken.

The ear is also almost all cartilage, except for the fleshy lobe. It consists of two bowls – the outer, flatter one forms most of the flap of the ear, while the inner bowl is deeper and leads into the canal. This is bounded in front by a little flap. There is a great variety of ear shapes, and the best way to become familiar with this complex little structure is to stand in front of a mirror and practise drawing your own two ears.

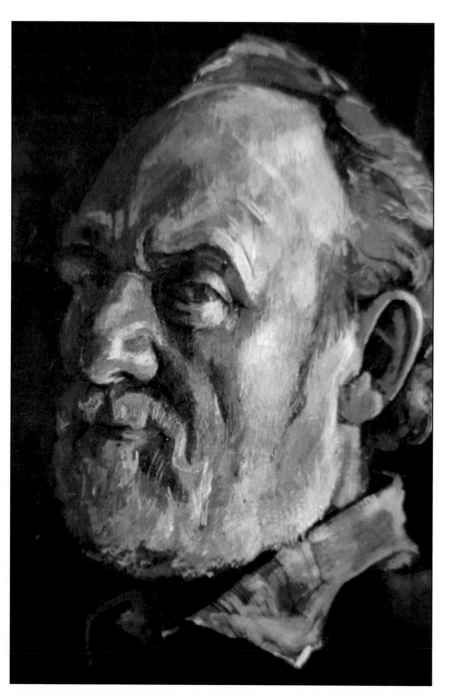

LEFT In this self-portrait in oils by the painter John Arnold there is a terrific sense of the volume of the skull, and the hair and beard have a structure that follows the form of the head and the facial muscles. The initial paintwork was quite broad, but the final paint layers were applied with smaller brushes in an almost crosshatched technique. A build-up of planes has been preserved throughout. Note the deep furrow down the side of the nose and the side of the mouth, caused by the elevator muscle. The large masseter muscle can be felt under the beard. The structure around the eye, with the emphasis on the brow and cheekbone, is beautifully described, and the eyelids perfectly follow the form of the eyeball. The ear is clearly and simply defined. The cartilaginous nature of the nose is very noticeable, and here reflected light has been used to good advantage.

9

ARMS, HANDS, AND FEET

The arm is a remarkable structure, especially the forearm. The radius bone can revolve around the ulna, which is hinged to the upper armbone, or humerus, and turn the hand almost 360°. A complex series of muscles in the forearm is involved in this action, and in the flexing and extending of the thumb and fingers. To help your understanding of this, extend the left arm with the palm uppermost, and place the fingers of the other hand on the crest of the ulna and the thumb in the hollow of the elbow. That group or bunch of muscles now held by the hand are the ones involved in bending the fingers in a gripping action. The group on the outer side of the arm not held are involved in extending the fingers outwards as well as twisting and turning the hand.

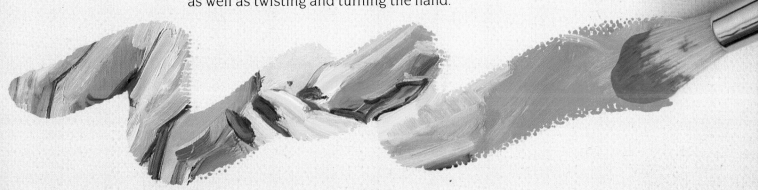

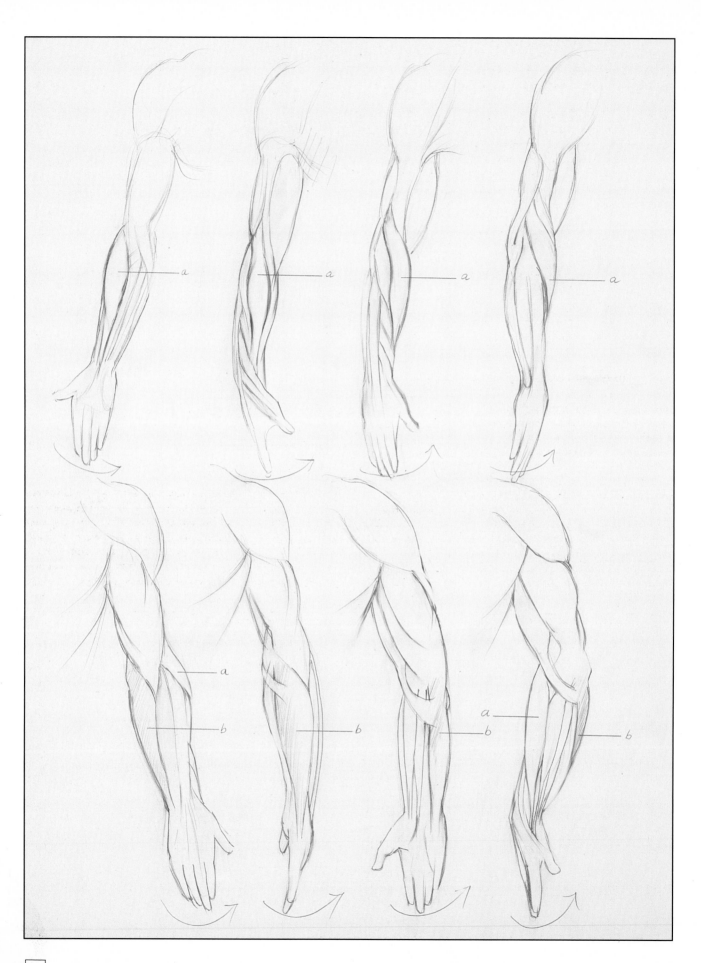

LEFT The technical term for turning is supination: look at the full figure on page 47. The long supinator was shown giving the arm much of its characteristic shape. The top row (left) shows the right arm with the palm open. Twisting the thumb inwards, towards the body, in the direction of the arrow, note the position of the supinator (a) as the thumb almost completes a circle. In painting the arm, which of course will assume many positions, it is important to observe and imagine what this muscle is doing in any position. It will be the greatest help in describing the structure of the arm. Looking from the back (bottom row), the muscle giving the characteristic form is the ulnar flexor of the wrist (b), which travels from the elbow to the wrist. Note how this muscle behaves in the turning arm, and also the position of the supinator (a), which is just visible initially but reappears prominently when the arm has turned fully.

BELOW Hands and feet often frighten the beginner as well. Here the most important thing is to simplify the problem by concentrating on planes. Trying to describe a hand, finger by finger, is asking for trouble, and often results in a bunch of bananas. First note a triangular plane that is made by the back of the hand, the first knuckle and the joint of the thumb. This is known as the *digital triangle* (a). Then it is useful to think across the knuckles, a line called the *transverse arch* (b). See the back of the hand as another plane (c), and take a line across each of the finger joints to give fundamental planes (d) and (e).

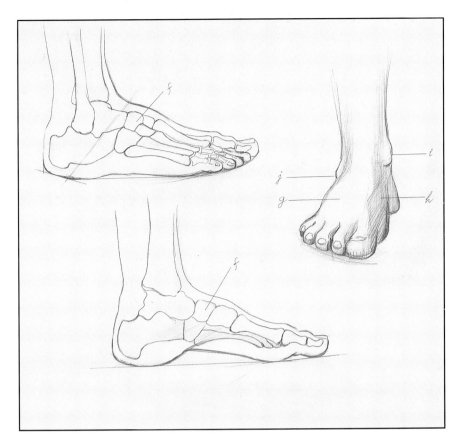

ABOVE The most common fault when painting the foot is to make it too much of an L-shape, with a sharp angle from the leg to the top of the foot. In fact, the top of the foot comprises a mass of seven bones called tarsals (f) — they correspond to the eight carpals in the wrist — and a flat tri-angular plane (g) falls away from the ridge caused by this group, down to the toes and outer side of the foot. By contrast, the inner side of the foot is an almost vertical flat plane (h). The protuberance of the ankle on the inside, caused by the tibia (i), is higher than that on the outside, caused by the fibula (j).

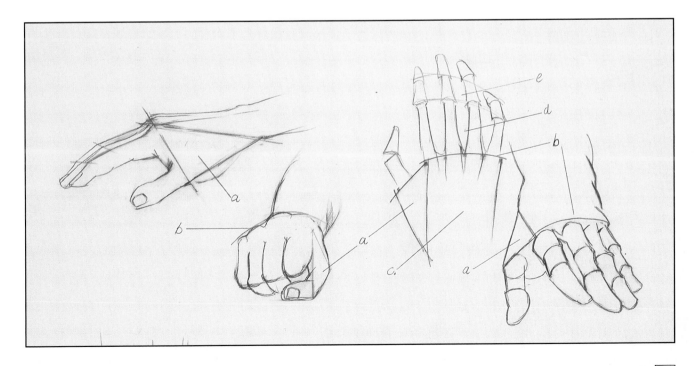

A PAIR OF HANDS

D A V I D   C A R R

The more practice you have at drawing and painting hands and feet, the better. You'll have no shortage of sitters if you use a mirror, and continual study will be repaid handsomely. This study was done in oils. The palette included French ultramarine, viridian green, cadmium lemon, yellow ocher, alizarin crimson, and titanium white.

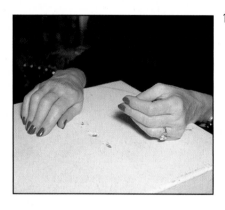

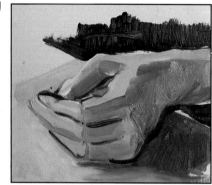

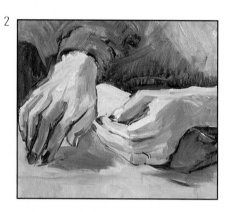

1 The model's hands were placed so that the light sources clearly illuminated the individual planes.

2 In this study the hand is established very simply in terms of planes. The digital triangle is there, and the fingers have been treated as a series of hinged planes. The colors used are yellow ocher and white, ultramarine and alizarin crimson. Some viridian is introduced to paint the table.

3 The second hand is included, and the table top painted more warmly. The plane at the wrist is made clear, and smaller planes within the fingers are defined with smaller brushstrokes. Cooler color is laid into the darker areas of skin.

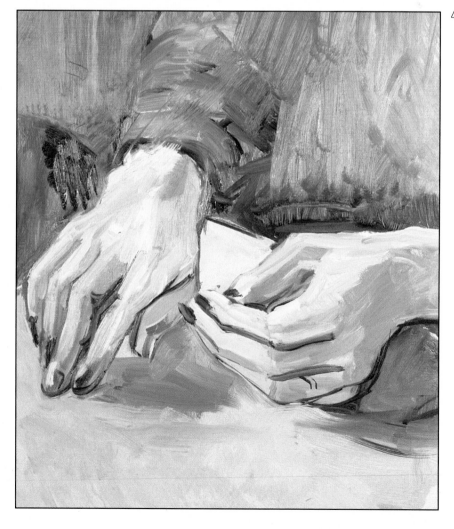

4 The basic aim is to see the hands as hinged planar forms, and to realize their structure clearly and boldly in this way.

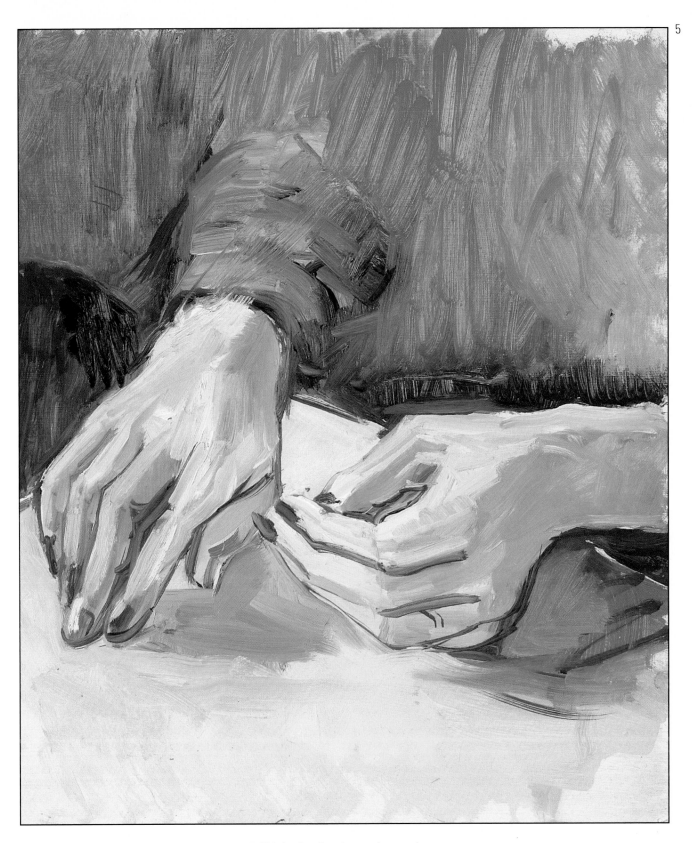

5 This basic *alla prima* study sees the brushwork following the directions of the form.

A PAIR OF FEET

D A V I D   C A R R

In this study, the artist decided to use a much thinner paint than in the preceding study, and also a different palette, which contained French ultramarine, viridian green, yellow ocher, raw sienna, cadmium red, and titanium white.

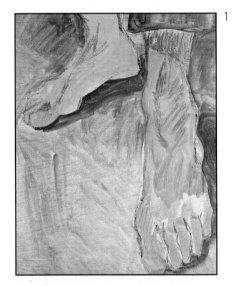

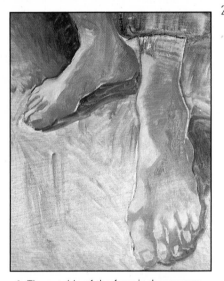

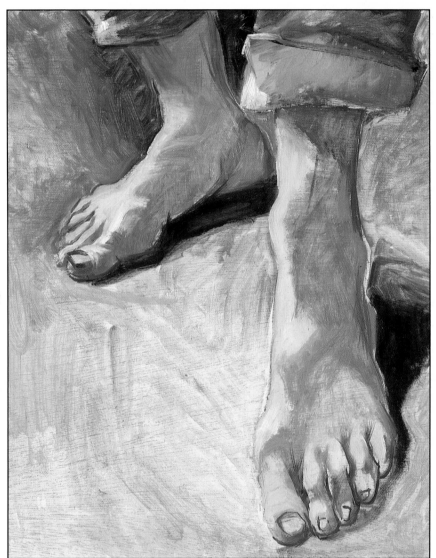

1 The outside of the form is drawn very simply in charcoal, and then the silhouette of the form is washed in with dilute yellow ocher. Try to be aware of the difference between the plane on top of the foot and that of the side. All other areas are washed in at this stage.

2 Some raw sienna with the slightest touch of ultramarine is scumbled over the yellow ocher for the darker tones. To preserve a clear change of tone at the ridge of the foot, white is added to yellow ocher to make the light planes clearer still.

3 The darkest parts of the feet, around the toes and heel and on the leg, have a further layer of ultramarine and sienna scumbled over them. Finally, some linear drawing is done around the toes. The technique of lightly scumbling darker, cooler paint over warmer, lighter paint, allowing some of the warmer paint to show through, gives a good sense of light on the flesh.

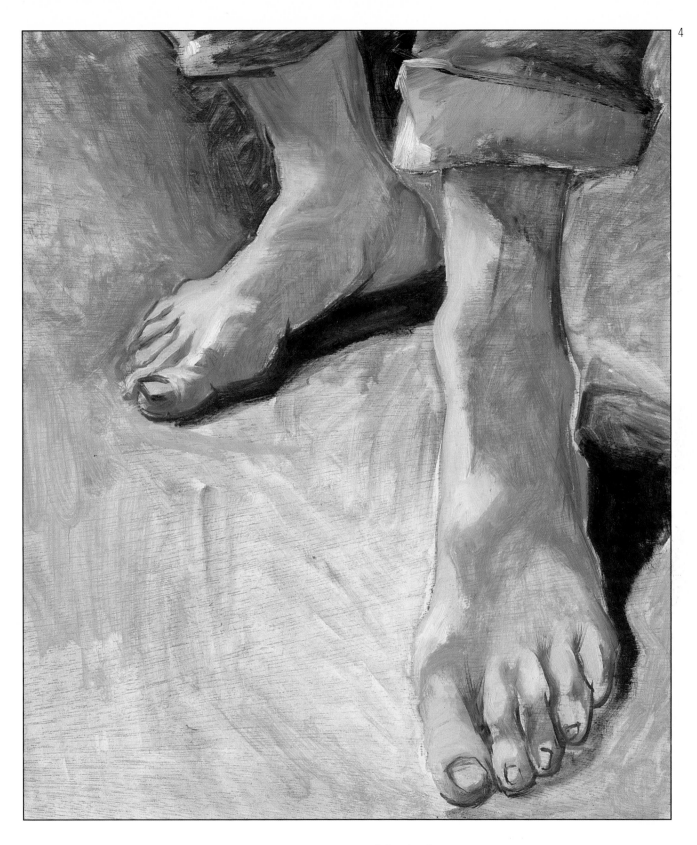

4 Note the strong sense of directional light from left to right, which just catches the leg of the jeans and casts a shadow over the ankle.

10

SKIN COLOR AND TONE

Paint manufacturers have produced a color that should be avoided at all costs. Its name is "flesh pink," and it is sometimes called "flesh tint." Its appearance is more akin to that of a cosmetic or dermatological cream, and it has no use whatsoever in the rendering of the luminosity of human skin. In the wide spectrum of skin colors, from the whitest of northern skins to the blackest of African skins, from Middle Eastern hues to the porcelain tones of the Far East, nowhere is this color found except in the circus.

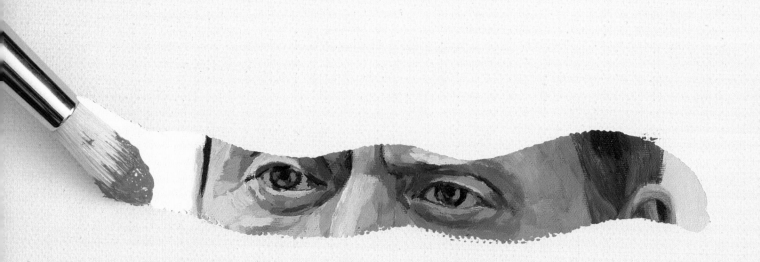

Many different factors are at work creating skin color and tone. Not only is skin color affected by the ambient light, but very much by the surrounding colors, and particularly clothing. Its variety results from racial origin, and degree of exposure to the sun and weather. It varies from one part of the body to another. Look at the flesh painted by the contemporary painter Lucian Freud. Ruddier skin is caused by the closeness of the blood vessels and capillaries to the skin's surface. In very pale-skinned people, the blue veins can sometimes be observed just below the surface.

There is a great variety of cool and warm skin colors and tones, and it is important to use warm and cool colors to the full when painting. Warm primaries include cadmium yellow, cadmium red and French ultramarine, and cool primaries lemon yellow, alizarin crimson, and cobalt blue. Earth colors, used carefully, are important. These should include yellow ocher, raw sienna, raw umber, and light red.

Careful use of warm and cool colors is a help in modeling the form, as cool colors tend to recede and warmer colors to come forward. It is also necessary to expect the interaction of complementaries to give a sense of light on and in the skin. Glazing darker colors over light and vice versa can give a real sense of luminosity. The scumbling of darker paint over light, allowing just a little of the underlying color to show through, gives a sense of light in the shadows. Renaissance artists frequently used a cool underpainting of green, gray or violet, over which they placed warm complementary colors. Very early Italian paintings often display this green appearance where the upper layers of paint have worn away.

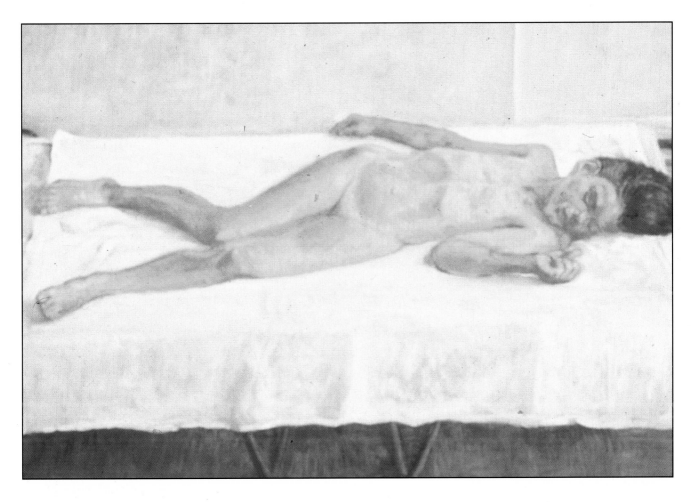

ABOVE In Victor Willis's painting of a young girl asleep, a very restricted palette has been used. The medium was oil, and the palette consisted of light red, yellow ocher, raw sienna, raw umber, and just a touch of cobalt blue and French ultramarine. Flake white was used throughout. It was executed over a period of several weeks. The overall skin tone was painted using Indian red and yellow ocher mixed with flake white. Darker tones were achieved with a light scumbling of delicate blue and raw umber. The consistency of light was maintained by the same treatment on the wall and sheet. Note how warmer Indian red mixed with raw sienna was used on the more exposed parts of the figure, such as the model's lower legs and arms.

SKIN TONES ON THE FACE AND BODY

These six paintings demonstrate how the color of skin can vary dramatically, depending on the light. Facial skin can be quite different from the skin on the body. In each painting the use of complementary colors are important in creating the form of the figure or face.

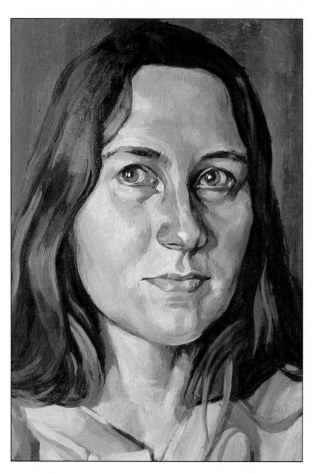

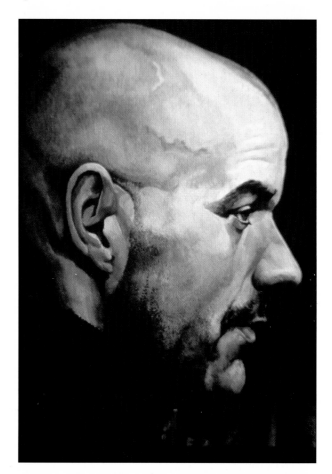

ABOVE LEFT John Arnold's portrait in oils uses more of a glaze technique. The artist began with an underpainting of strong colors, which were gradually muted by lighter glazes of subtle yellows, pinks, grays, and blues. The glazing medium was a 50/50 mixture of dammar varnish and turps. He used warm and cold primaries: bright red, winsor yellow, cadmium yellow deep, yellow ocher and French ultramarine being warm; and rose madder, lemon chrome, winsor blue, cold.

ABOVE RIGHT AND RIGHT This dramatic portrait in oils by John Arnold uses the same palette. This was not glazed at all, but painstakingly built up using thin impasto, with careful attention to the planes and color modulations. It was mostly painted using hog-hair brushes, but fine detail was achieved with small sables.

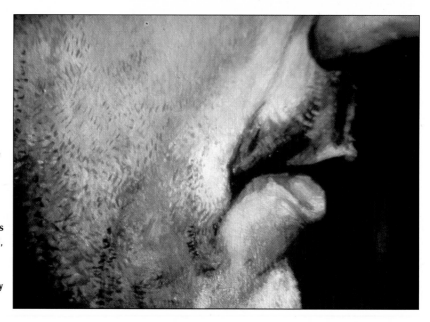

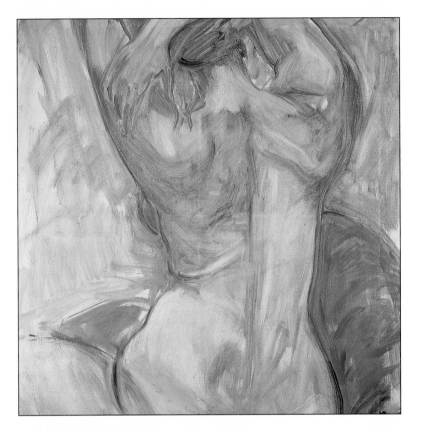

LEFT There's an altogether different approach in Kay Gallwey's oil painting of the back with raised arms. The artist used rags and fingers to paint with, as much as brushes, and we can see how her marks flow around the forms. Working on a warm-toned ground and with lots of turps as a medium, she has established most of the flesh with raw sienna and umbers, into which she has introduced cool pinks and reds and complementary green for the darker tones.

BELOW LEFT AND RIGHT Kay Gallwey adopts a similar approach in her watercolors, and in both pictures of the girl in the black hat she uses large brushes to modulate warm yellows to cooler pinks, defining and redefining the form with sepia. Notice how she likes to place her figures within an interesting setting. The busy textures and patterns and strong colors act as a foil to the simpler areas of flesh.

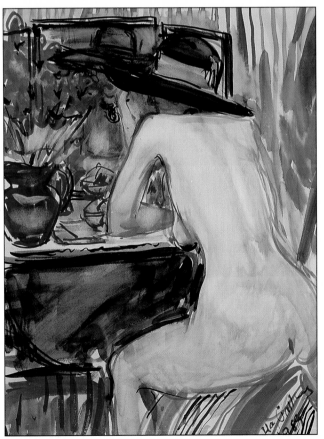

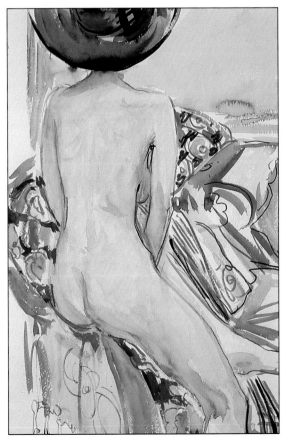

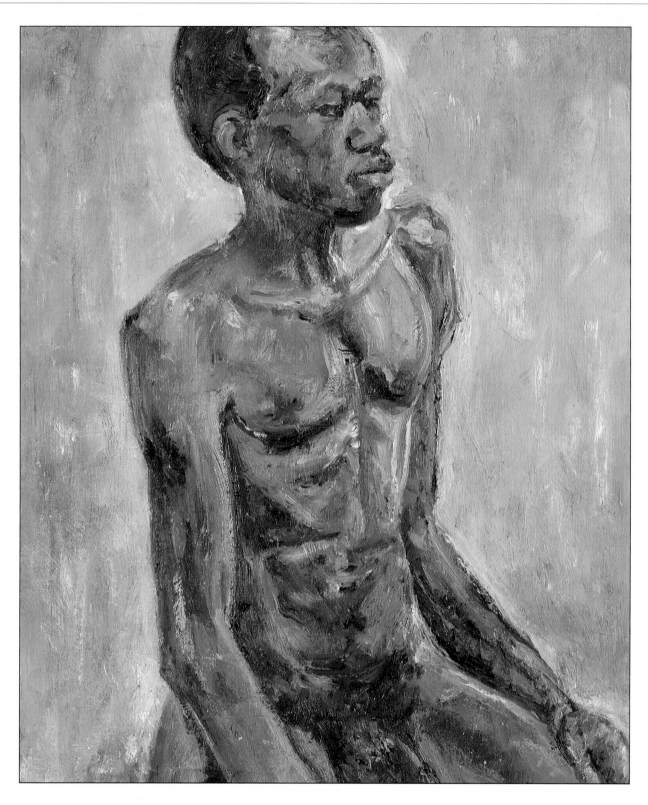

ABOVE In this portrait in oils, the artist, Irene Lightbody, began on a warm-toned ground with an underpainting of dark colors – raw sienna, alizarin crimson, and French ultramarine. The dark pigmentation of black skin means reflected light is much more noticeable, and this can be cool and bluish or warm and yellow. Within the skin itself there is a wide variety of colors – a mixture of Vandyck brown and yellow ocher simply doesn't work. Strong blue and green accents have been seen and stated boldly, and these work effectively with the golden yellow and warm reds. The blue paint scumbled over the warm ground behind the figure provides an effective contrast.

CONTRASTING SKIN TYPES

There are three very different types of skin represented in these paintings. Even within a relatively small area of skin, there are many subtle changes of color.

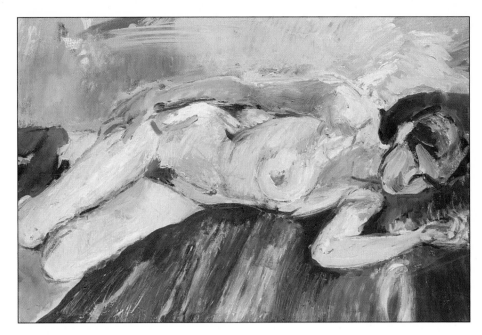

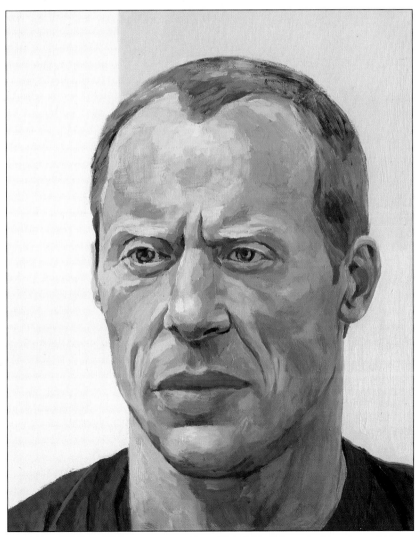

ABOVE This oil painting of a reclining figure by the author was completed at one sitting. It is *alla prima* throughout. Beginning with a simple base of warm color using cadmium yellow, cadmium red, yellow ocher, and white over a strong linear drawing of French ultramarine and raw umber, the artist worked into it using thicker paint and a loaded brush. Alizarin crimson, ultramarine, and some viridian green are applied freely into the wet paint to give darker, cooler tones. The large areas of dark cloth and the black socks contrast well with the flesh, and the dramatic orange of the upper arm modified by blues and greens acts against the slab of blue paint on the floor. Some of the later paint was applied with a palette knife.

LEFT This portrait head in oils by Judith Symons is of special interest as earth colors formed the predominant part of the palette, plus a little cadmium lemon and mineral violet. The palette consisted of oxide of chromium (a dull green), Vandyck brown, raw sienna, Venetian red, cadmium lemon, mineral violet, and titanium white. The artist shows how many subtle changes of color can occur within a relatively small area of skin. It was painstakingly painted with a careful, analytical approach. She used small, square sable brushes with a thin impasto, using a little turps to make the paint flow, but taking care to let her brushmarks stand. This gives clarity to the planes and a good sense of structure to the head.

11

TWO APPROACHES TO PAINTING THE FIGURE

It is worth studying two contrasting approaches to the figure. One shows the painter concerned solely with the image of the figure. There is little interest in the figure's relationship to space, and the figure usually fills or almost fills the canvas. This approach was generally followed by Amedeo Modigliani (1884–1920) and might loosely be termed the "Modigliani syndrome." The other convention might be called the "Giacometti syndrome." Alberto Giacometti was an Italian-Swiss painter who spent most of his life in Paris, and his work is characterized by an obsessive interest in the figure placed in space and its relationship to the position of the painter and the surrounding objects; but more of that later.

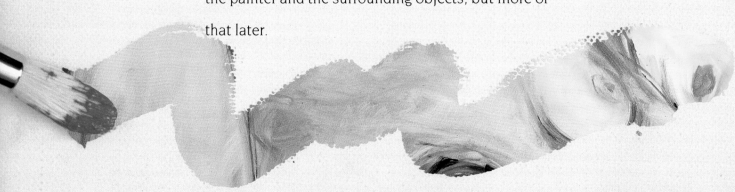

THE FIGURE FILLS THE PICTURE

Modigliani's early work was very much influenced by Cubism, which led to his characteristic image of the elongated neck and the graceful long oval forms of his later work. His paintings of the nude fill the whole picture area, often spilling out so that only the head, torso, and pelvis fit the frame. There is little depth, the simple forms behind the figure suggest a very shallow picture space.

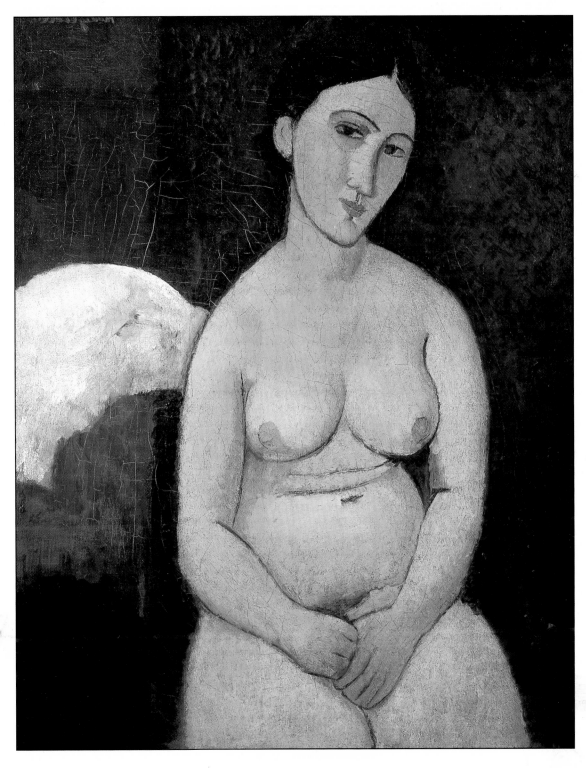

A B O V E **The massive forms loom large in** *Seated Nude* **(1917) by Modigliani, as if the artist was very close to the model.**

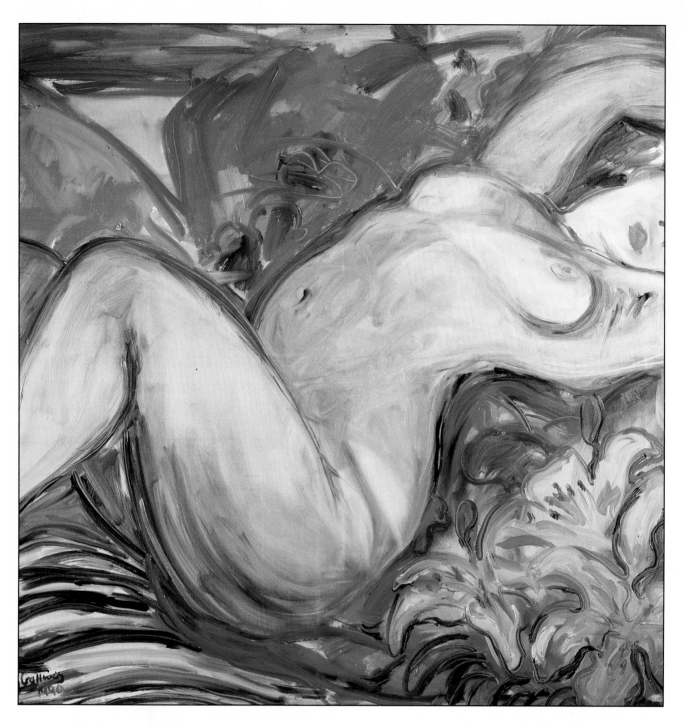

ABOVE **A large and energetic, reclining nude in oils by Kay Gallwey.**

This large nude in oils by Kay Gallwey is a good example of the Modigliani approach. The figure is flung backwards over the couch and out of the picture. Recessional space is unimportant. The artist's working method is worth noting. She uses a standard palette of hot and cold reds, blues, and yellows with a permanent green and viridian green. She uses very little earth color.

Usually she will be working on a primed white canvas. Her medium is a 50/50 mixture of genuine turpentine and refined linseed oil. Much of the painting has been done using soft cotton rags wrapped around the end of the finger. In this way she can maintain a bravura approach and can infuse the picture with energy.

First she dips the rag in the

medium and mixes it with warm yellows and reds, and lightly masses in the main areas with quite fluid paint. She is able to wipe off this paint easily in order to create transparency and let the white canvas impart luminosity. She is careful not to lay down any warm colors where there may be a need for cold areas (patches of blue). She adds more paint using the rag, modeling the form in a very direct way as if the fingers were touching the flesh itself. Lighter areas are

BELOW **This technique can be seen to very good advantage in her picture of the back of a girl arranging her hair. Again the paint is applied freely with finger and rags. Although there is more concern for space, as the figure is reflected in the mirror beyond, nonetheless there is a strong sense of a flat jigsaw pattern of shapes dividing up the picture surface. Note again the use of muted green and crimson in the flesh, and the effective contrast of the warm yellow-brown arm against the gray-violet of the reflection.**

achieved by rubbing out. More sumptuous color is reserved for the drapery. Note the touches of green shadow in the flesh around the ribs and under the breasts. This is particularly effective against the complementary red of the cloth. Cooler viridian green and alizarin crimson are applied under the thigh.

Brushes are used in the final stages of the painting – notably in the strong pattern of the foreground cloth and finer lines under the breast and around the thighs.

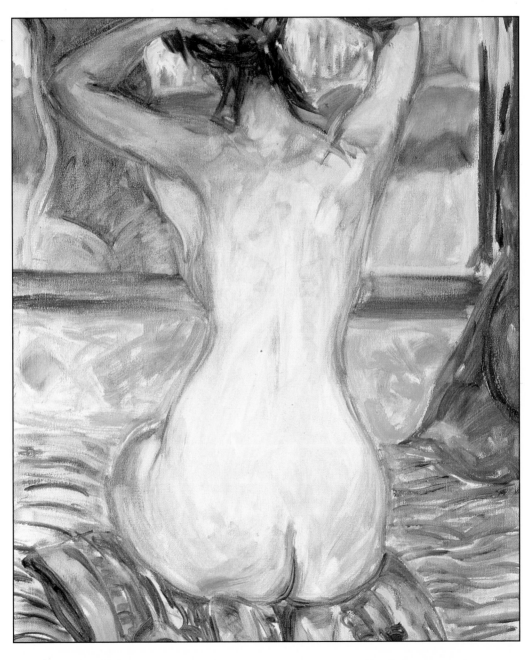

THE FIGURE AND SPACE

For Alberto Giacometti, the figure's real existence in light and space is crucial. Most of his working life as an artist was spent trying to bring his image alive. He called it making it "like" – not a copy or likeness – but reaching that moment when the painting or sculpture jumped into life for a split second. It was this search that led him to the elongated and narrow forms of his sculpture, to seemingly incomplete forms. He felt that as he "finished" a figure, it lost its spark of life.

Working on a flat canvas, he did everything he could to create a sense of real space inhabited by a real form. His paintings are more a record of this search than a finished statement.

Giacometti's portrait of Annette (1954) is typical. He is really trying to see the figure "appearance" size, not larger or smaller, and this involves placing the figure in space precisely at its actual distance from the painter. This problem of size and distance drove him to distraction. "An arm is as vast as the Milky Way, and this phrase has nothing mystical about it. The distance between one wing of the nose and the other is like the Sahara, without end, nothing to fix one's gaze upon, everything escapes," he said.

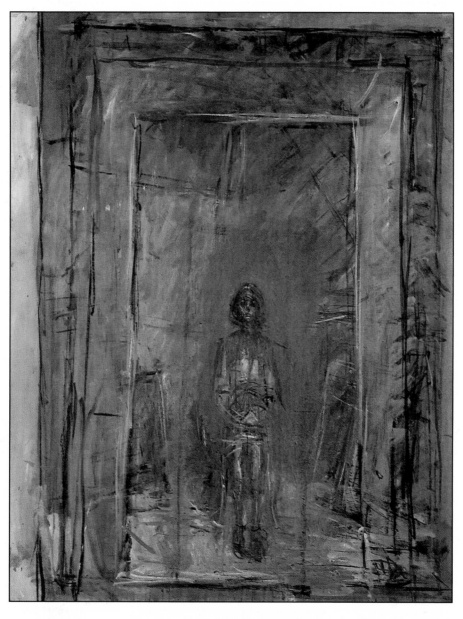

A B O V E **In *Annette Assise* (1954) by Giacometti, the figure is set back in space, pushed there by the illusory painted borders like multiple window-frames. His** whole working process can be seen on the canvas – marks are painted in and out, and all the time relationships between figure and space are established by actual lines of black, gray, white, and ocher moving between the objects through the space. At the heart of this space is the central core of compressed form – the head.

The figure here, painted in oils by the author, is sitting in a light-filled room. Various colored curtains change the color of the light coming through the windows. At the top of the picture in the far corner of the room, cooler daylight streams through. The figure traces a diagonal from corner to corner. The predominant colors in the triangle above this are cool, cerulean blues, lemon yellows, cool pinks, and lilac. The lower triangle comprises rich velvety oranges, warm violets, and reds. The figure against the blue areas tends to be orange, and the thigh against the warm chair and floor is a very cool light lemon and cerulean. Consciously or otherwise, all these relationships have to play a positive part in creating the sense of a light-filled space.

In technical terms, the initial drawing involved an awareness of all the points of intersection of the space and the figure. In other words, just where did the carpet intersect with the knee? Where did the lines of the windows, floor and walls, if extended, pass through the figure? This is another way of setting up relationships.

The palette was quite extensive: French ultramarine, cobalt blue, cerulean blue, viridian green, raw umber, cadmium lemon, yellow ocher, cadmium yellow, cadmium red light, and alizarin crimson. Thinner underpainting in base colors is built on wet into wet with progressively thicker paint, until much of the final layer is scumbled and scratched over the surface, allowing previous layers of color to shine through.

BELOW **The large studio space was exploited here in this oil painting of a seated figure.**

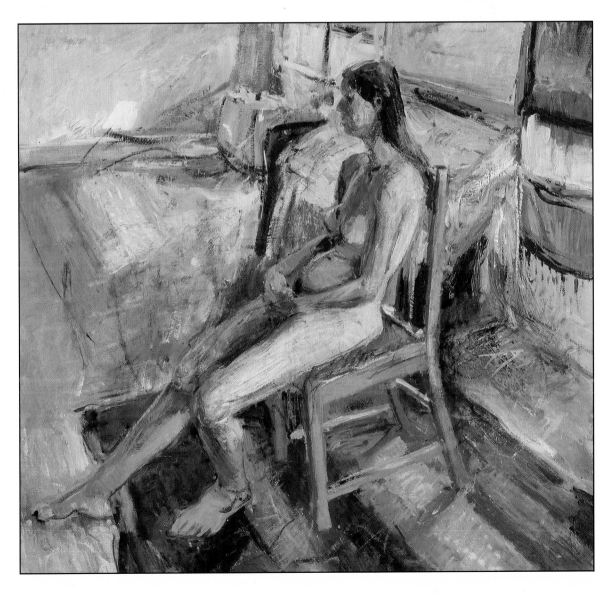

12

TONAL PAINTING

On several occasions in this book the term "restricted palette" has been used. It is important to realize how much can be achieved with economical means. A restricted palette can mean anything from three or four colors – for example, titanium white, yellow ocher, raw umber and French ultramarine, which would be ideal for tonal studies – to earth colors enlivened by one or two primaries, to the three primary colors, or any other combination where the decision has been made to keep the color strictly limited.

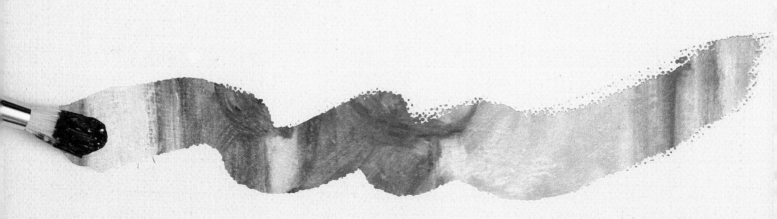

RESTRICTED PALETTE STUDIES

Painting with a restricted palette is often a useful economy but, as these paintings demonstrate, it can also be a good discipline. It requires the artist to concentrate on establishing the right differences in tone, from light to dark, without the freedom of a full range of colors.

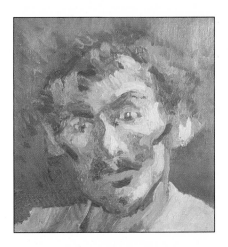

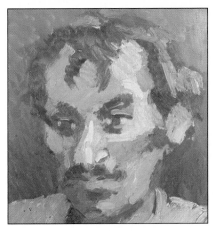

ABOVE Mike Knowles's restricted palette used for these two portrait heads in oils was raw umber, raw sienna, Indian red, cobalt blue, Prussian blue, and black. The paintings were worked on weekly a number of times, and scraped back between each session. They were each completed finally in one session *alla prima*. A restricted palette can be extended, and in this case some viridian green, cadmium red, yellow, and lemon were used sparingly. The blue/ green of the wall behind the head acts as a foil to the flesh, which was painted using various combinations of light red, raw sienna, and white. In the portrait with the tilted head, touches of cadmium red on the forehead and cobalt blue down the side of the nose and forehead push the form around, and there is a terrific unity in the painting achieved by the positive brushwork over the whole surface. The second picture has bold planes of light raw sienna down the side of the forehead, on the cheekbone and down the side of the nose, with a deeper sienna used for the rest of the face. The darker tones under the eyes and around the chin are made with black and cobalt blue with touches of sienna. There are warmer accents on the ear and lip.

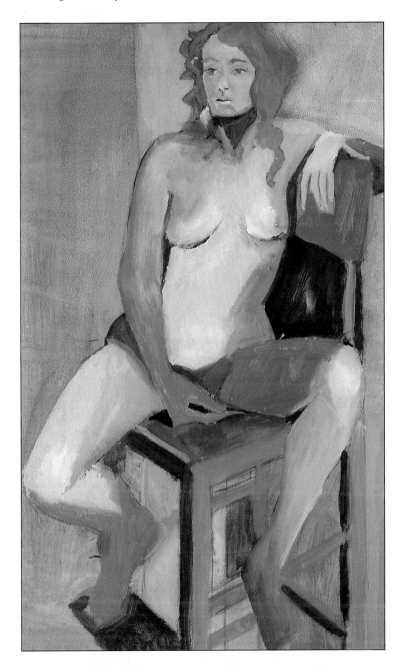

ABOVE This seated figure, in oils, is a good example of tonal painting using a restricted palette. Painted on a warm ground, yellow ocher and white depict the brightest and warmest light, and pure yellow ocher the next tone down – the hair, part of the hip, and the model's right foot. Then raw umber lowers the tone further with touches of French ultramarine, notably on her right arm and inside left thigh. More ultramarine was introduced for the darkest areas. Taking this approach, the artist has made decisions involving simplified forms and planes, and at what tone and temperature to pitch each part on a scale from the lightest, warmest ocher to the cooler, darker tones.

SEATED WOMAN

J O Y   S T E W A R T

The restricted palette for this sequence is yellow ocher, cadmium red light, alizarin crimson, French ultramarine and titanium white, plus an occasional cooler lemon yellow.

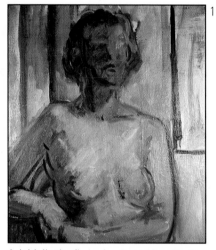

1 Initially the figure is massed in with thin alizarin crimson, into which are worked mixtures of cadmium red, yellow ocher, and white.

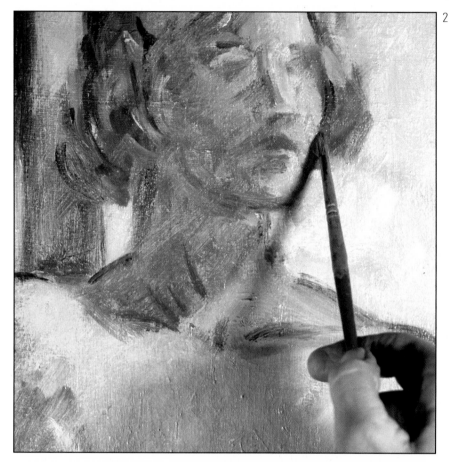

2 This is drawn into with lines of pure ultramarine and alizarin crimson.

3 The form is built up, establishing the strong light plane of the torso with more yellow ocher and red, and placing accents of light yellow ocher on the breast. The darker areas are built up with a light scumble of ultramarine, which is particularly effective around the side of the face. Some reflected light is observed on the breasts, and is picked out with ultramarine and white. A strong form has been achieved with great economy of means. The light works well. There is some very fluid drawing around the arms, and the clear, directional brushwork in the torso makes for a convincing study.

4 A solid and imposing result, using a restricted palette.

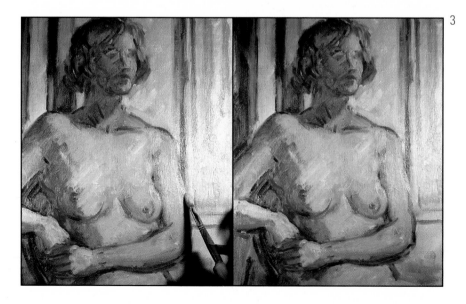

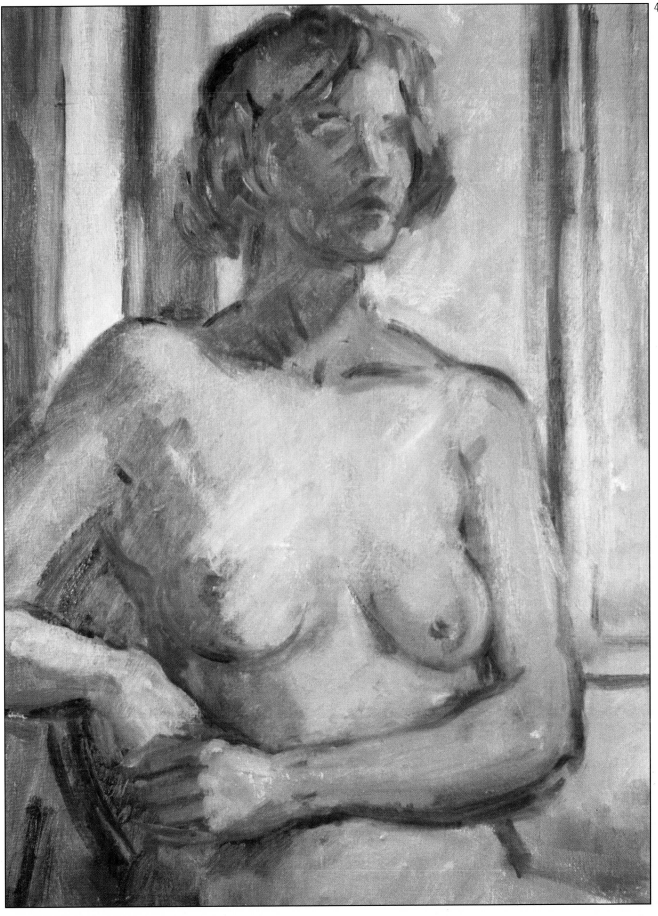

13

LIGHT AND COLOR

"Light cannot be reproduced, but must be represented by something else, color. I was very pleased with myself when I found this out." This simple but crucial statement was made by one of the pivotal figures of late 19th- and early 20th-century painting, Paul Cézanne (1839–1906). Although painters of the 19th century were increasingly interested in the growing scientific research into the field of color, artists have always known that a sense of light is created by a juxtaposition of colors. There are Pompeian wall-paintings full of golden light and lavender shadow; green shadows complement the warm carnation of the flesh in early Italian painting; yellow and violet are used as primary components of color chords in medieval glass.

Sir Isaac Newton's experiments with the prism and demonstration of the components of white light (the spectrum) were to increase this awareness of color and its properties. Eugène Delacroix, in the early 19th century, said his starting point as a colorist came from observing the rainbow and looking at the flesh of Rubens's Nereids in *Marie de Medici landing at Marseilles* in the Louvre, Paris. In his *Massacre at Scios* he introduces hatchings of pink, orange-yellow, and pale blue into some of the flesh. His

experiences in North Africa in 1832 and the impressions of light and color he received there were a crucial influence on his later work, just as they were for Henri Matisse in the early 20th century.

In the same year (1832), the French chemist Eugène Chevreul published a paper on color theory which asserted that "any color in isolation is surrounded by an aureole of its complementary". Among many notable achievements, he invented margarine and lived to the age of 103. In 1824 he was

appointed director of the dyeing department at the Gobelins tapestry factory in Paris, and in 1839 produced his most influential book, *Of the Law of the Simultaneous Contrast of Colors and the Assortment of Colored Objects*.

From Delacroix onwards, the influence of scientific color theory allied to the artist's natural observational skills is clear. Impressionism, Post-Impressionism, and Fauvism all relied heavily on the behavior of complementary colors.

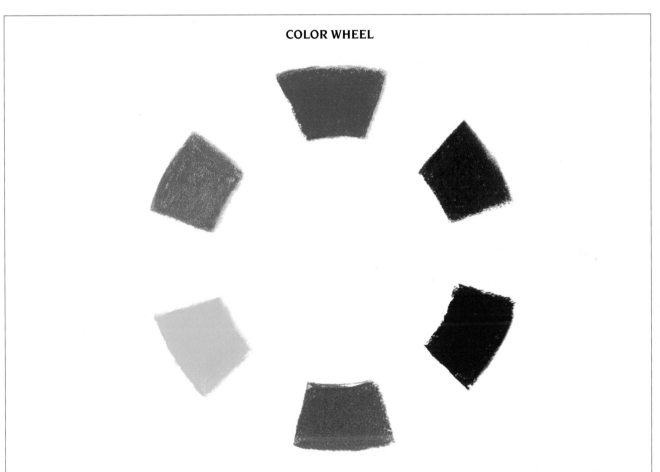

COLOR WHEEL

ABOVE At the top of the circle is a primary red. Immediately we encounter the vexed question as to what constitutes a primary red, or any other primary color for that matter. There have been many attempts to fix the primaries, but suffice it to say that primary red must come somewhere midway between orange on the one hand and violet on the other. The three primary colors are red, yellow, and blue. They are called primary because they cannot be made by taking any other colors and mixing them. The primary colors can be warm or cold. Red is not automatically a warm color – it can be cool as it moves towards violet (eg., alizarin crimson), or warm as it moves towards orange (eg., cadmium red light). A cool yellow would be lemon, and a warm one cadmium yellow deep. Cerulean blue is cool as it moves towards green, and French ultramarine warm as it moves towards violet. The colors between the primaries are called secondaries, and each is produced by mixing two primaries. The secondary colors are green, violet, and orange. The fun really begins with complementaries.

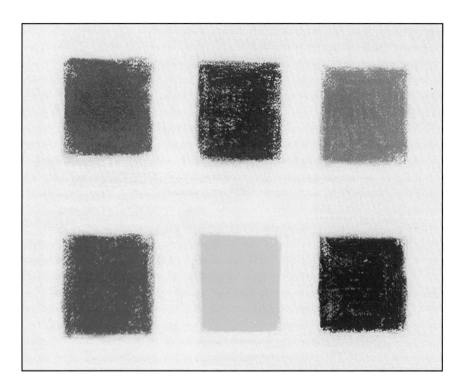

ABOVE The complementary of any primary color is the result of mixing the other two primaries. So, in the column of colors, the complementary of primary red is green (primaries blue and yellow mixed), the complementary of primary yellow is violet (red and blue), and the complementary of primary blue is orange (red and yellow). They are diagonally opposite each other in the color circle.

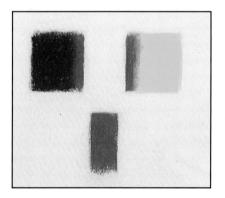

ABOVE The small diagram shows why certain colors, when mixed, give another color. Colored dyes and pigments appear the colors they are because they absorb all color wavelengths except one, which they reflect. The reflected wavelength is perceived as the pigment's color. However, this is a simplification. In the example, blue and yellow each contain a little green. This is not normally noticeable as it is not the dominant color or wavelength. When they are mixed, however, blue absorbs the yellow light, and yellow absorbs the blue, and their common denominator, green, now doubled, is given off and picked up by the eye.

Thinking again about light, we realize, as Cézanne did, that we cannot copy the brilliance of light itself with our relatively dull pigments. Even the strongest colors are inadequate, and if we resort to the addition of white to increase their brilliance we merely tend to make them chalky. It is through the interaction of colors and their juxtapositions that we can begin to create equivalents for light. Only then can we hope to place our figures in situations of convincing light and space, and to paint flesh with any kind of luminosity.

To do this we need to know about primary and secondary colors, which for convenience are usually represented in a color circle.

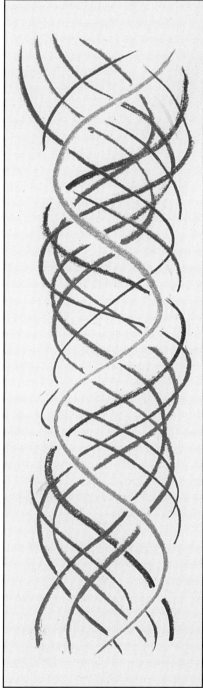

ABOVE In proximity, complementary colors enhance and enliven each other. Another experiment undertaken by Chevreul when he had problems producing a vibrant blue dye for the tapestry industry is illustrated by the "twisted thread." He took several strands of blue (all slightly varied) and introduced a strand of orange – the complementary. The yarn produced had specks of orange in it. The eye perceives the blue as being more intense than it actually is because of the presence of the complementary.

IMPRESSIONIST APPROACH

It is well worth while taking account of these discoveries in your own work. By deliberately trying an Impressionist or Fauvist approach, you can assimilate some of their techniques and enliven your own work in the process. It can help to avoid a tendency to rely too heavily on earth colors when painting flesh, for example, or to resort to brown and black when wishing to make things darker. Instead, you will be able to create shadows that contain light, and play off the figure against its surroundings.

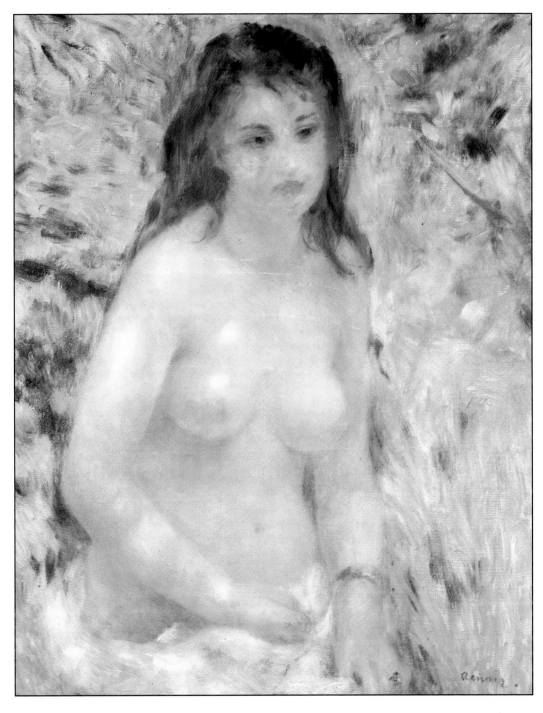

ABOVE In Renoir's painting *Woman's Torso in Sunlight*, the figure is bathed in dappled sunlight. The figure is surrounded by foliage, and we assume that the light is filtering through the leaves and branches above. The face is much warmer than the porcelain-like flesh of the body. This whole effect of light is achieved by exploiting warm and cool complementary color contrasts. Yellows and pinks play off against hints of blue and green over the surface of the flesh itself, and the subtlety of the figure contrasts well with the more boldly painted landscape.

GIRL LEANING ON PILLOWS

KAY GALLWEY

This oil painting relies mainly on the delicate contrast of yellow and pale lilacs, pinks, muted green, warmer yellows, and cool blues.
The palette is French ultramarine, cerulean blue, viridian green, oxide of chromium, cadmium lemon, cadmium yellow mid, cadmium red, and alizarin crimson, thinned with turpentine.
The brushes used are a no. 5, no. 8 square, a no. 8 round bristle, and a large, round, long-handled hog-hair.

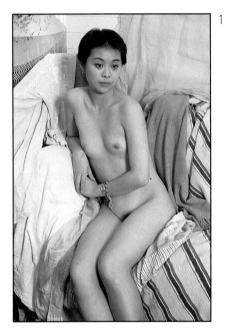

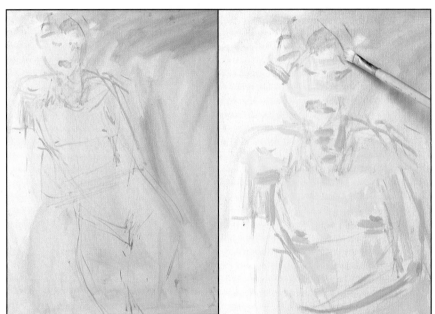

1 The model was seated against a number of cushions.

2 The study is painted on a canvas with a warm cream ground. The artist does the preliminary drawing with a fine brush and alizarin crimson. With a rag, she works crimson behind the figure and cerulean blue around it, and begins to paint into the figure with cadmium yellow.

3 She supports her arm with a maulstick rested on the canvas at one end, and begins to define the head with violet (alizarin and ultramarine) using the large hair brush. She introduces much stronger accents into the drapery, and a striking crimson pink at the figure's shoulder.

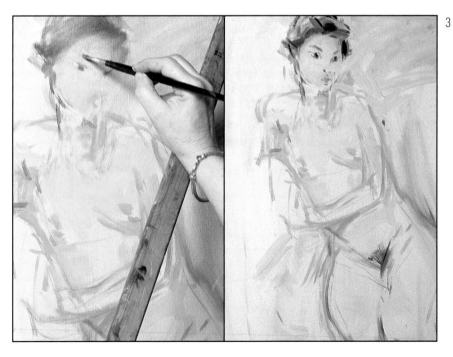

4 The artist takes great care with the axes of the body. There must be a strong sense of the model's right arm bearing the weight and pushing up at the shoulder. She places a clear line at the "hinge" there. She continues to develop the drapery as it will be crucial in creating the rhythmical and fluid contour of the figure. She works more light, warm yellow paint into the body, and cooler paint above the breasts.

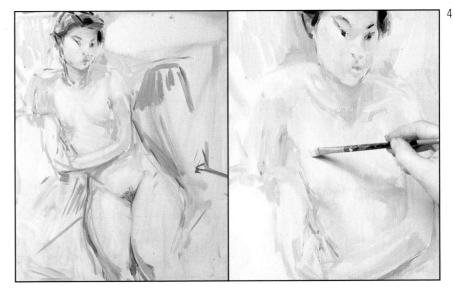

4

5 She builds up the color in the face, and begins to introduce some delicate complementary green to the forehead, around the neck, and under the elbow. The green used is oxide of chromium mixed with white.

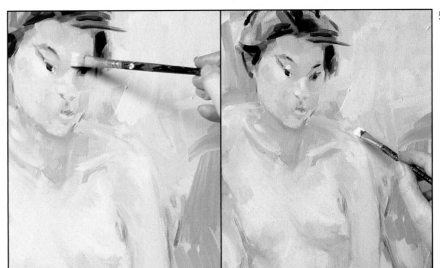

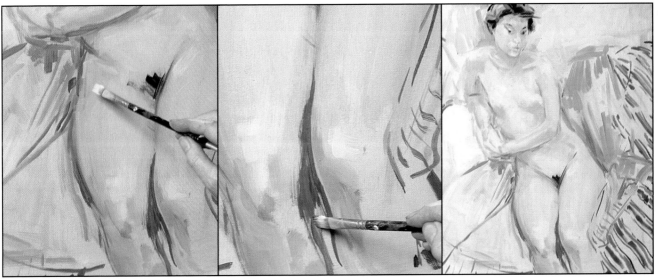

6 She begins to develop the form of the figure further by painting into the shadows. She has wiped away some of the paint with rags, and in the detail the cream ground can be seen clearly. It is, in fact, being used here as a color in the painting. Toned grounds such as this can have a terrific unifying effect within a picture.

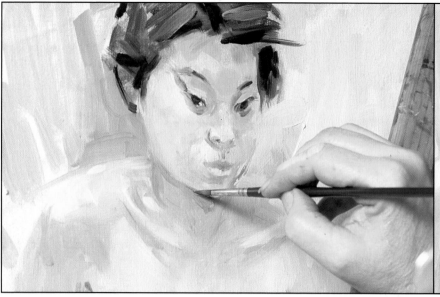

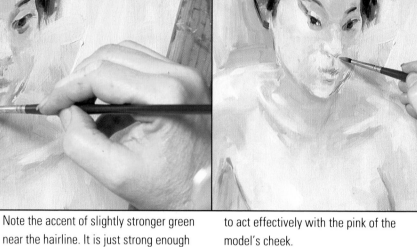

7 With the most delicate touches of dull green and violet, she defines the face.

Note the accent of slightly stronger green near the hairline. It is just strong enough

to act effectively with the pink of the model's cheek.

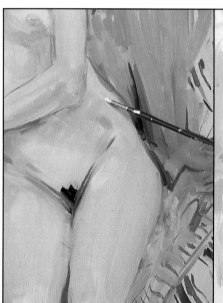

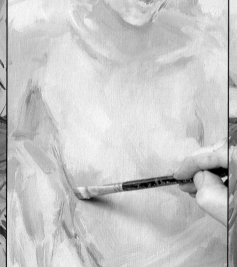

8 Refining work takes place on the body, building up a sense of luminous skin. Subtly modulated strokes of pink and lilac gray play against the predominantly pale yellow flesh.

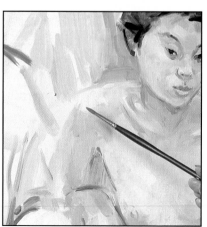

9 A strong highlight is placed on the shoulder to give an added sense of pressure at this point.

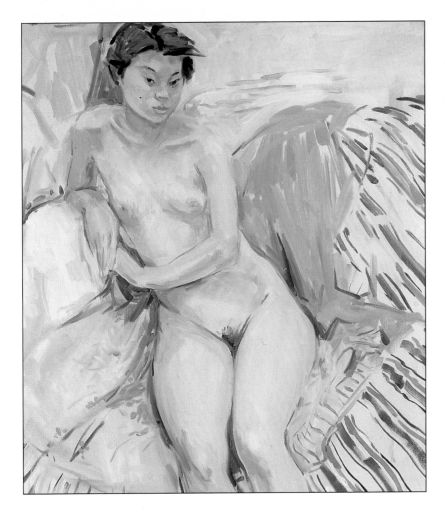

10 The volume of the pink sheet behind the figure becomes more solid, separating the figure from the busy striped cloth on the right. The turquoise cloth is enlivened with touches of pure orange. The drawing of the hand and arm is completed. The feeling of light has been skillfully created by a carefully balanced use of complementaries: delicate green against pink, lilac against yellow, and the warmer yellow against blue.

OIL STUDY USING STRONG COLOR AND THICK PAINT

In this large painting of a reclining figure by the author much stronger color has been used. It is 5 × 4 ft (1.5 × 1.2 m) on canvas. The initial layers of paint were laid in flat with plenty of turps, and were worked into with thick paint of tube consistency. Very little mixing was done on the palette, and many different strokes and swirls of paint were applied with both brush and fingers. The palette is a fairly simple one of titanium white, two blues (French ultramarine and cerulean blue), two yellows (cadmium lemon and cadmium yellow mid), two reds (cadmium red and alizarin crimson), and viridian green. Blacks have been made with a

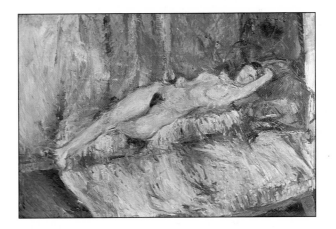

mixture of alizarin, French ultramarine, and viridian green. The flesh is treated more simply than the highly textured paint surface of the drapery. A light cadmium yellow and red mixture has had a variety of colors scrubbed into it – warmer reds on the lower leg tucked under

the body, warmer yellow on the stomach, and cooler lilac and violet touches on the thigh, breasts, and face.

A B O V E **This whole painting has a tapestry-like feeling, with strands of color weaving together to give a sense of light.**

FAUVIST APPROACH

Just as the term Impressionism was culled by a newspaper critic from the title of a painting by Claude Monet, so the Fauves ("wild beasts" in French) received their name from the critic Louis Vauxcelles at their now-famous exhibition of 1905. Fauvism was a relatively short-lived and loose movement of artists without formal theories or manifestoes that existed during the first years of the 20th century, but it has been profoundly influential.

Color was liberated to operate as a language in its own right, more akin to music. Indeed, the whole business of manipulating color can be likened to striking chords and discords. Matisse was to say later, "Thus it is that simple colors can act upon the inner feelings with all the more force because they are simple. A blue, for instance, accompanied by the shimmer of its complementaries, acts upon the feelings like a sharp gong. The same with red and yellow; and the artist must be able to sound them when he needs to."

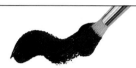

WOMAN SEATED BY RED SCREEN

KAY GALLWEY

The model is seated against very bright fabrics to give the artist full play with color. Only a few colors have been used, and the palette comprises French ultramarine, cerulean blue, cadmium lemon, cadmium yellow deep, cadmium red, alizarin crimson, and ivory black. It is painted on white primed canvas tacked to a board.

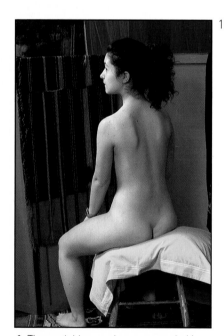

1 The model is seen here surrounded by strong primary colors.

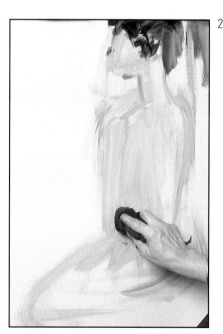

2 Three slabs of color are put down – the stripe of ultramarine along the top, part of the red screen, and cadmium yellow for the body. With a rag dipped in turps, the artist moves the paint around on the canvas.

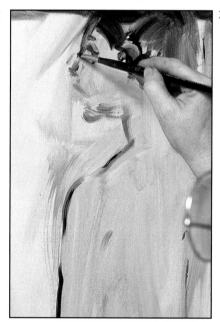

3 With ivory black she lays in the hair, and begins to draw the face, neck and arms, working into the wet yellow paint and allowing them to mix.

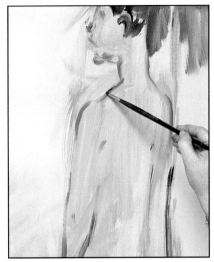
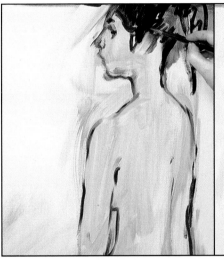
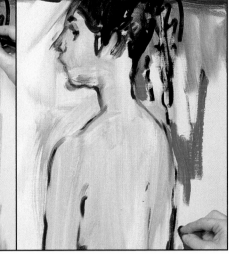

4 More of the body is drawn with black and cadmium yellow deep.

5 The artist works stronger black lines into the hair, and has drawn some of the figure in ultramarine. Much stronger, purer color is now applied – a powerful red around the head.

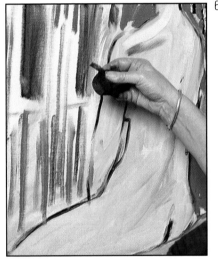
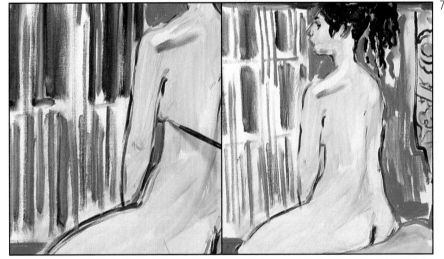

6 The artist extends the red into the cloth to the left of the figure. Then, taking a rag dipped in turps and a mixture of alizarin crimson and ultramarine, she daubs in the fabric.

7 At this point she introduces some fluorescent day-glo paint into the picture to make things really go with a zing. With a no. 5 round bristle brush, she draws multiple contour lines around the form in bright red and green.

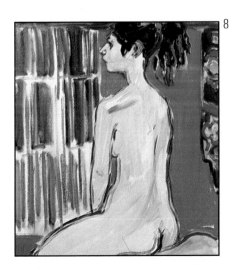

8 She uses some of this color in the face, and places some strong accents of a fluorescent blue in the hair, at the same time completing the patterned cloth on the right.

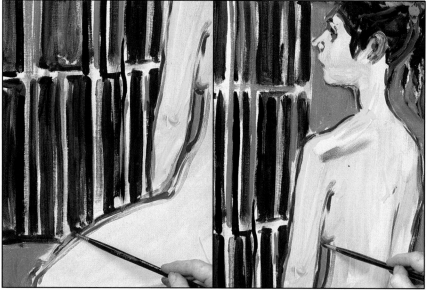
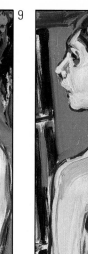
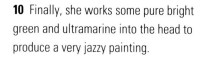

9 The artist makes the cloth darker, and continues to modify the contour with a darker line of deep violet. She paints a lot more lemon yellow, cadmium yellow deep, and light cerulean blue into the flesh of the head, neck, and body.

10 Finally, she works some pure bright green and ultramarine into the head to produce a very jazzy painting.

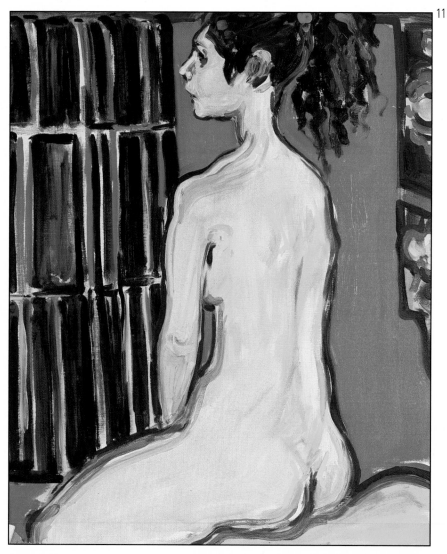

11 Strong, bold color and rapid execution are the keynotes of this vibrant study.

FAUVIST STUDIES

These two oil studies are both examples of a Fauvist approach. In each case, the resulting painting is a strong statement in bold colors.

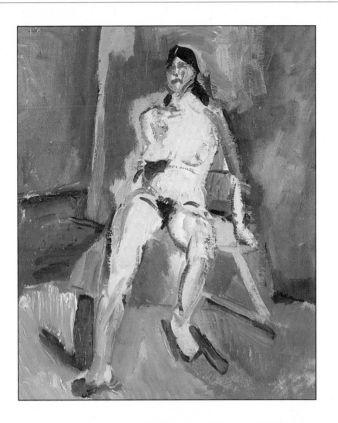

LEFT This painting has been achieved with primary colors only. It is oil on canvas, and the palette is manganese blue (a slightly more powerful and greener blue than cerulean), lemon yellow, cadmium yellow, cadmium red, and alizarin crimson. The green wall behind the figure contains various mixtures of yellow and blue, the floor mixtures of cadmium red and manganese giving a brownish-violet tinge. White has of course been used in the figure. The base color is cadmium lemon and white, into which slabs of warmer yellow have been worked on the upper chest and the figure's right thigh. Into this stronger drawing, marks have been worked using a deep violet mix to carve out the form.

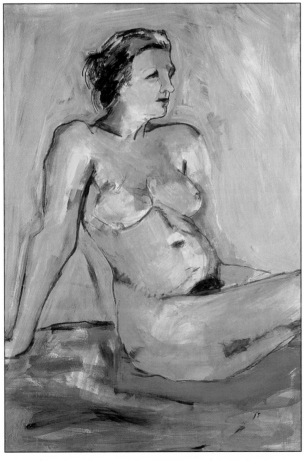

LEFT Working over a warm ground, the artist, Marie Wylan, has successfully contrasted this monumental figure with the blue wall behind. The warm ground shows through the blue, and the base color for the figure is also warm, with colder color applied on top. The palette was French ultramarine, viridian green, cadmium lemon, cadmium yellow, cadmium red, alizarin crimson, and titanium white. The form of the figure has been described with a large, square brush in light alizarin, and over this have been laid strokes of cadmium lemon, tinged with green. Some of the warm cadmium yellow base at the figure's left shoulder, her stomach and hipbone has been left to give a sense of volume and of light coming into the picture from the right.

RAPID WATERCOLOR STUDIES

These four studies can also be termed Fauvist in approach, with their use of areas of strong color and the clear linear definition of the figure.

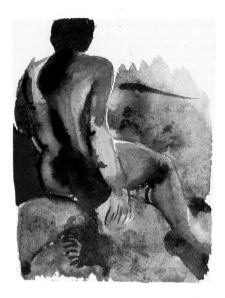

BELOW These three small watercolors by the author, painted rapidly at one sitting, have a calligraphic quality about them. Strong blocks of pure color have been laid down for the figure and space, and allowed to bleed a little. There is some glazing, but the form is fully defined by dark, sweeping lines of deep violet (alizarin crimson and French ultramarine) or a near black (cadmium red and French ultramarine).

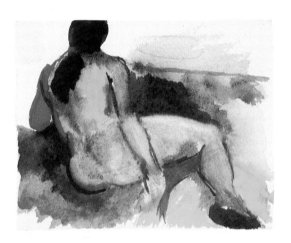

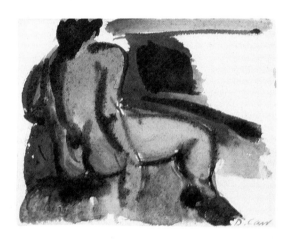

LEFT Similarly, in the small reclining figure by the author, broken washes and glazes of clear, warm and cold colors gain their definition by drawing in the form.

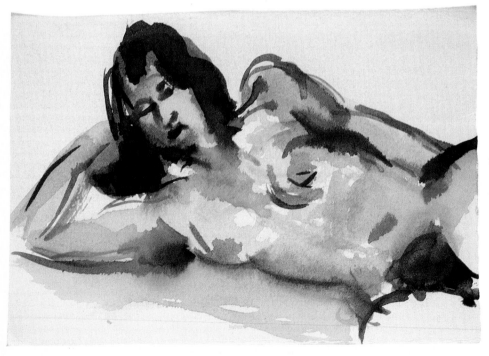

14

OIL GLAZE TECHNIQUE

The use of oil glazes, layers of thin, transparent paint, is the most traditional of all oil-painting techniques. Unlike *alla prima* or wet-into-wet painting, which is usually completed in the space of a few hours, or days at the most, the glaze technique needs a longer time scale and some careful planning. This considered approach has been used since the time of van Eyck (1390?–1441), and in one form or another is the foundation of the work of painters up to the end of the 19th century. Painters do still work in this way today, but it is no longer the norm.

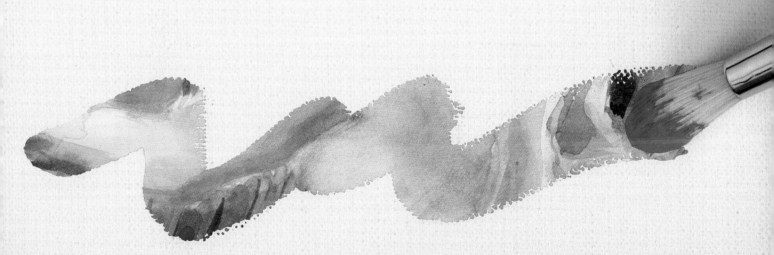

The development of open-air painting, the invention of the oil-painting tube, and the desire for the greater immediacy that the Impressionists favored saw the growth of *alla prima* techniques. Van Gogh is a fine example of this bold and direct approach to painting, working with a fully loaded brush and impasto. A late 20th-century painter like Frank Auerbach scrapes off much of the previous day's work and paints the image afresh with luscious and thickly applied paint.

Nonetheless, many contemporary painters feel that the oil-glaze technique ideally satisfies their own particular needs. It is not as complicated or as mysterious as some people think, and is an important addition to the technical repertoire. Even if you do not use it fully, it is a useful introduction to the use of glazes, which can play an important part in any painting in its later stages.

The technique involves an initial drawing in charcoal, or an underpainting in neutral colors such as raw umber or the ochers. Some painters used gray, from which comes the term *grisaille*. Titian aptly called this stage of the process "making the bed of the picture."

When the underpainting is dry, color is glazed over it, layer upon layer, the paint being allowed to dry between each stage. Thicker paint, or impasto, can be applied at any time, and allowed to stand in its clarity or further glazed over.

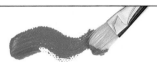

YOUNG MAN LEANING ON WINDOWSILL

MICHAEL CHAITOW

Planning is important. The figure was seated on a stool against a purple velvet cloth. The artist decided to work from the head and torso, and to fill the picture frame with the subject. He was interested in exploiting the dramatic light contrasts of the flesh and the velvet. An oil glaze technique is particularly suited to such dramatic tonal differences.
The palette used is raw umber, cadmium yellow, cadmium red, alizarin crimson, rose madder, winsor violet, and titanium white.

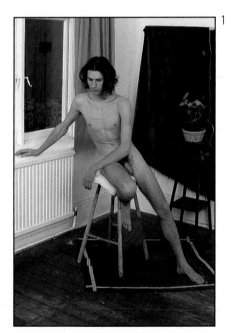

1

1 The model in position.

2 Working on a white ground, the artist draws in the basic shapes of the figure in charcoal. He has decided to use a water-based medium, gouache, for the underpainting in order to speed up the process. This is perfectly legitimate as normally he would have to wait for each layer of paint to dry thoroughly. The water-based underpainting will act in exactly the same way as an oil-based one would. If acrylic paint rather than gouache is used, it must be kept very dilute. He adds a small amount of acrylic white to the shoulder. He then fixes the drawing.

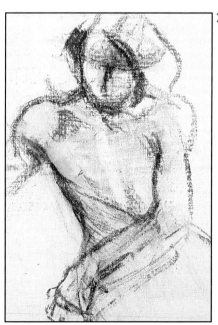

2

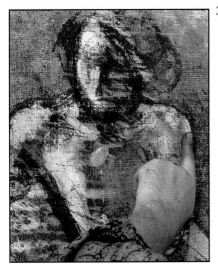

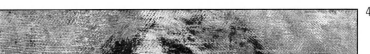

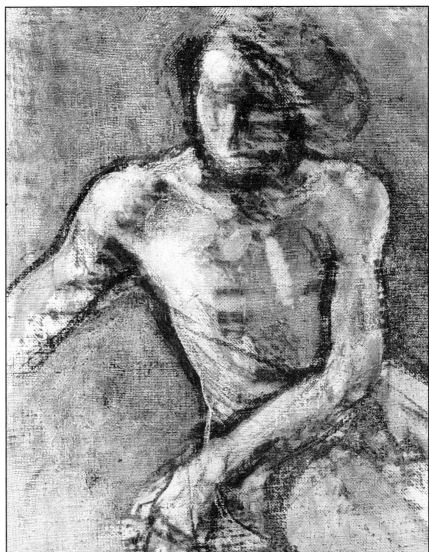

3 He now begins to strengthen the drawing, giving the figure much greater mass by pushing the charcoal around using both a cloth and his fingers. He uses a putty eraser to pick out some of the form.

4 The figure and its surrounding space are now well established and developed with charcoal, black and white conté, and white acrylic.

5 The artist clarifies the edge of the arm further with black acrylic. We can see how simply but subtly the form has been drawn.

6 Now comes the dramatic part – the application of a glaze. The glazing medium used here is made up as follows: one part stand oil, one part dammar varnish, one part genuine turpentine. The pigment in this case is a mixture of alizarin crimson, raw umber, and violet. The artist based this choice partly on the mood of the pose and sitter, and partly on the deep violet velvet cloth behind the figure. The glaze is applied evenly across the picture using a 1½ in (3.75 cm) brush.

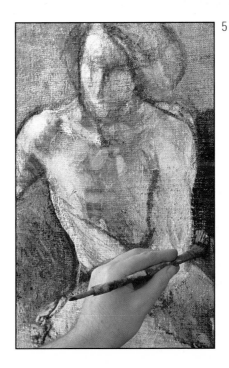

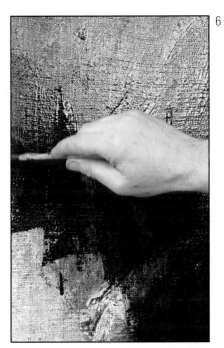

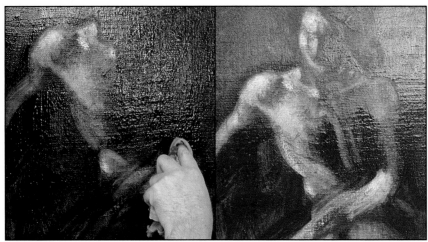

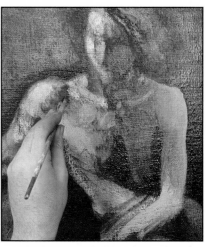

7 Taking a cotton rag, he rediscovers the forms of the figure by gently wiping away the glaze. He constantly refers to the model while doing this as adjustments of form can still be made. We can now see the charcoal drawing and underpainting.

8 Using a flesh tone mixed from cadmium red, cadmium yellow and white, he begins to paint some of the lighter flesh tones with a thin impasto.

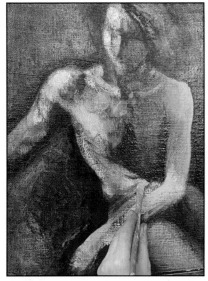

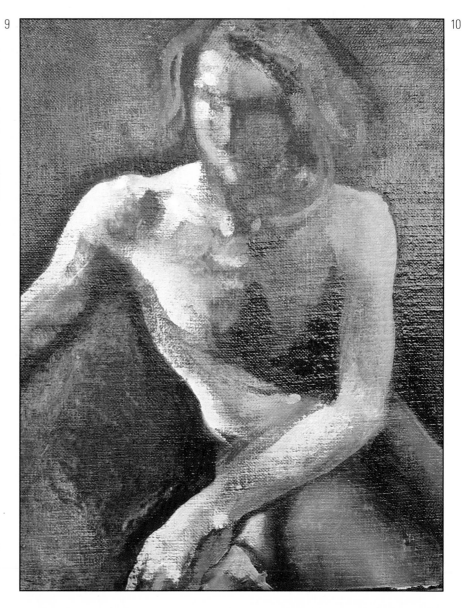

9 The artist uses stronger cadmium red and yellow to paint the warmth around the stomach, and he establishes striking highlights on the model's right shoulder, chest, waist, and wrist.

10 He blends the paint around the model's head, and places warmer accents on the forehead and left arm and hand.

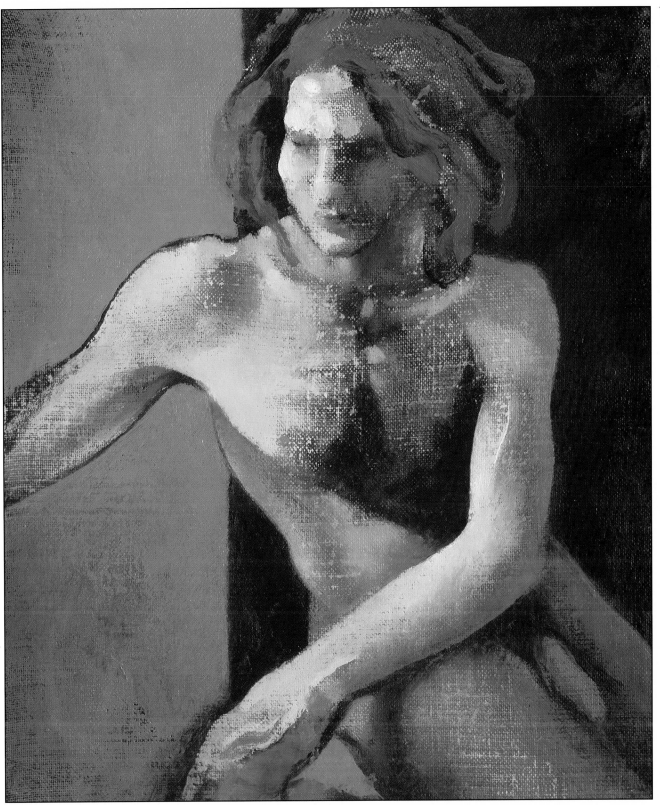

11 The final stage is painted at a later sitting, once the painting has had time to dry. He gives the painting an all-over glaze, again using a mixture of rose madder and raw umber, and wipes this off with a cotton rag to find the form. He continues to lay in opaque flesh tones. He develops the face and hair further, and makes a small alteration to the cloth on the side of the head.

GLAZE UPON GLAZE

These paintings are all examples of the use of oil glazes and they display the richness and depth which can be achieved using this technique.

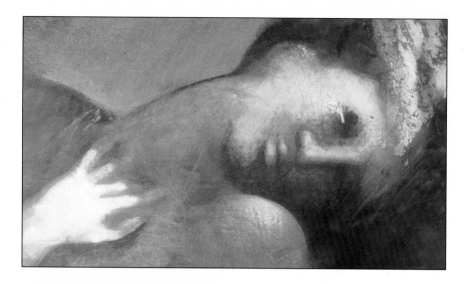

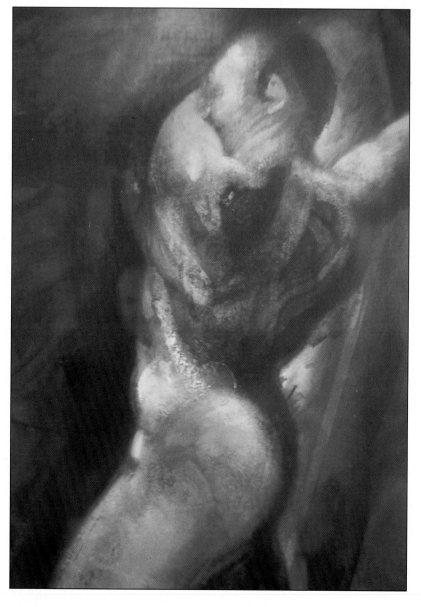

ABOVE In these finished studies by Michael Chaitow, the technique can be seen to full advantage. Glaze upon glaze of color mixed with the glazing medium, and carefully wiped off to reveal the form, gives a rich resonance to the pictures. Paint is scumbled over a glaze, over which the artist can glaze again, if necessary. Note the impasto around the woman's reclining head in this picture, which has had a further glaze laid on it. Deep, dark areas contrast dramatically with the highly worked lighter forms.

LEFT In this male torso by Michael Chaitow, glazing over the scumbled paint gives a great sense of the underlying power of the turning form.

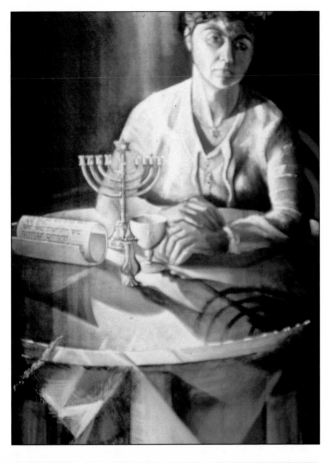

LEFT In this portrait, cooler glazes over warm give a beautiful sense of light and stillness.

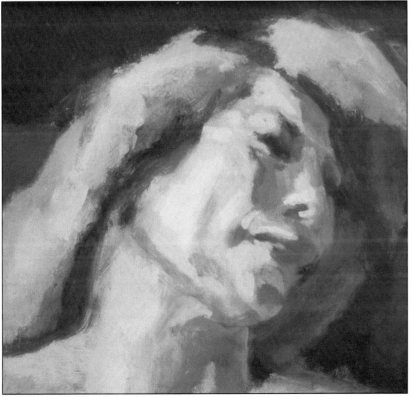

LEFT This painting by Mike Knowles has an underpainting of thin acrylic paint over a white acrylic ground. The model was lit powerfully from the side by an electric light. The basic painting of the flesh was laid in with Indian red and cadmium red, the deep space behind the figure with cerulean blue. Then glazes of Prussian blue and black were applied to the spatial area. The glazing medium is one part stand oil, one part dammar varnish, and one part genuine turps. The flesh and hair are glazed with thin mixtures of white and cadmium reds and yellows. For the darker areas of the skin, cobalt blue mixed with cadmium red and white has been used to give a gray violet. *Terre verte* (a transparent green) is used in the shadow under the hair.

15

WATERCOLOR GLAZE TECHNIQUE

W atercolor painting is often thought to be very difficult because once a mark has been made it cannot be changed. So you must "get it right" first time. To an extent this is true, but watercolor techniques can, in fact, be far more flexible than commonly supposed. The glaze technique involves building up layers of light washes, allowing each layer to dry before applying the next.

WOMAN SITTING BY A WINDOW

SHARON FINMARK

This painting demonstrates how a watercolor can be built up with layers of light washes, and how quite large changes can be made during its development. The palette is Prussian blue, French ultramarine, viridian green, lemon yellow, cadmium yellow mid, cadmium red, permanent rose, and alizarin crimson. The brushes used are nos. 10 and 12 sable nylon mix, a no. 3 sable and a 1½-in (3.75-cm) flat wash brush. A small natural sponge and blotting paper are also used.

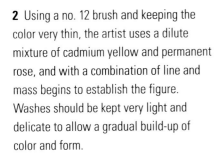

1 The model posed in front of the window.

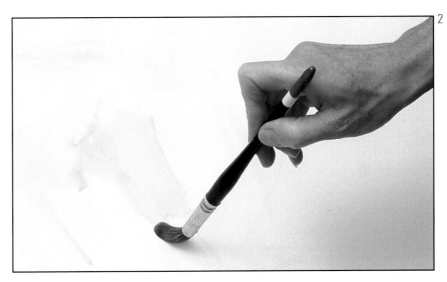

2 Using a no. 12 brush and keeping the color very thin, the artist uses a dilute mixture of cadmium yellow and permanent rose, and with a combination of line and mass begins to establish the figure. Washes should be kept very light and delicate to allow a gradual build-up of color and form.

3 The artist establishes the shapes around the figure using a neutral color (viridian and rose mixed). Complementaries mixed together always produce interesting neutral tints. Try mixing various reds and greens, blues and oranges, lemons and violets.

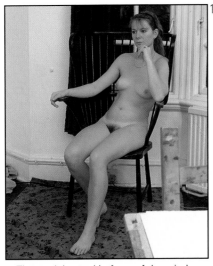

4 The chair and the window behind the model are established lightly, and viridian green has been used to describe the cooler shadow on the model's left arm and to define the form of the thighs.

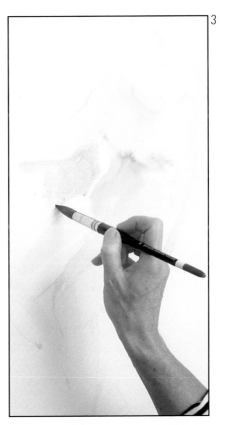

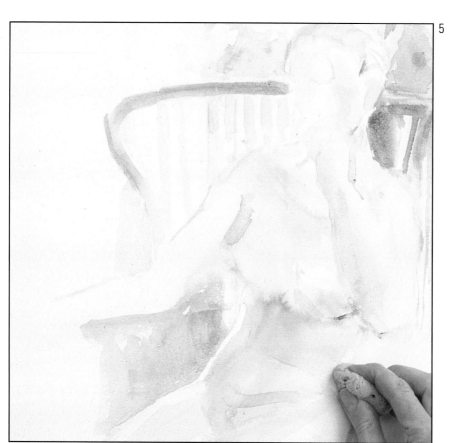

5

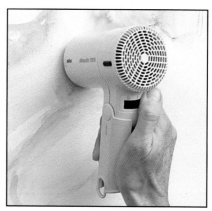

6

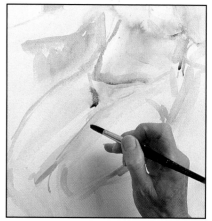

6 In order to control this, she takes a small hairdryer and quickly dries the areas she is changing.

7

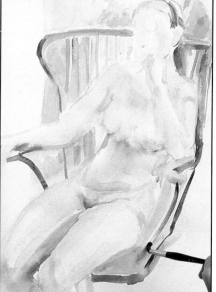

7 Now she can redraw the figure using French ultramarine and crimson.

5 Now we can see how quite important and necessary changes can be made. The artist feels that the marks down the side of the figure are too strong and impinge too much on the form. The form is defined too strongly in general. She is unhappy,

also, about the position of the figure in the chair, and wishes to move it – pretty drastic modifications. Taking a small sponge dipped in clear water, she wets the surface and sponges off the color on each side of the figure.

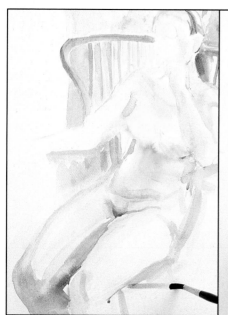

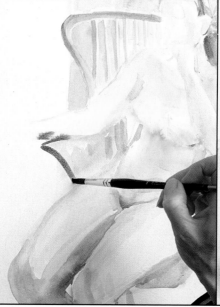

8

8 She begins to establish the lower legs and the shape of the chair, and uses some

cadmium yellow to bring out the warmth of the chair seat.

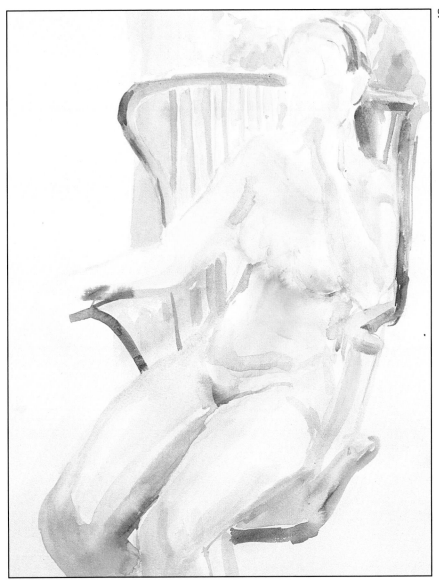

9

9 Note how in the whole scheme of things the lemons and cadmium are acting against the violets and blues.

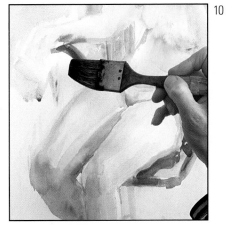

10

10 Using a 1½-in (3.75-cm) flat wash brush, the artist begins to lay in the wall and the curtain.

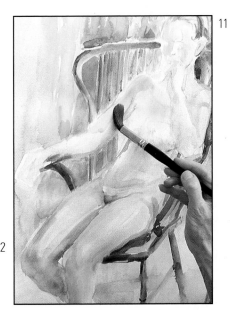

11

11 Using a large sable mix brush, she lays in the figure more strongly, glazing transparent orange over the completely dry layers beneath.

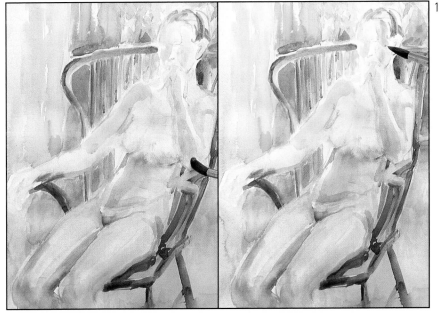

12

12 Here we see she has warmed up the whole figure, as she felt it had become too violet. Note, too, the strong glaze of green along the figure's left thigh, which acts effectively against this warmth.

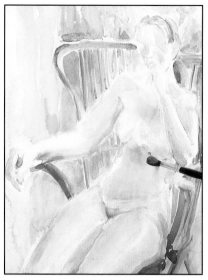

13 She is unhappy about the strength of the red patch beneath the breasts, and takes a brush with clear water to dampen this area and blot it out.

14 The paint has been removed and, with blotting paper in one hand, she takes a fine sable brush and begins to define the face and the breasts.

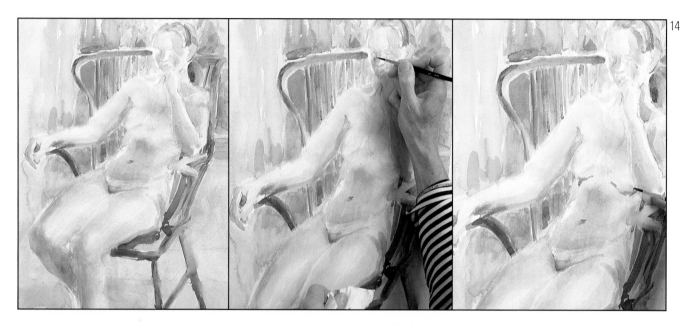

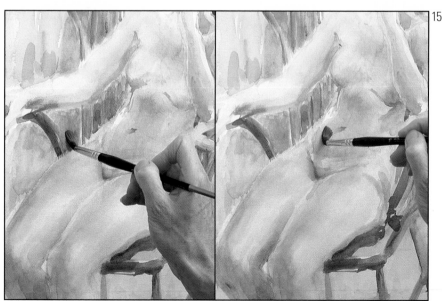

15 Finally she strengthens the wall behind the figure with a further glaze, and emphasizes the form of the stomach, introducing some green under the breasts.

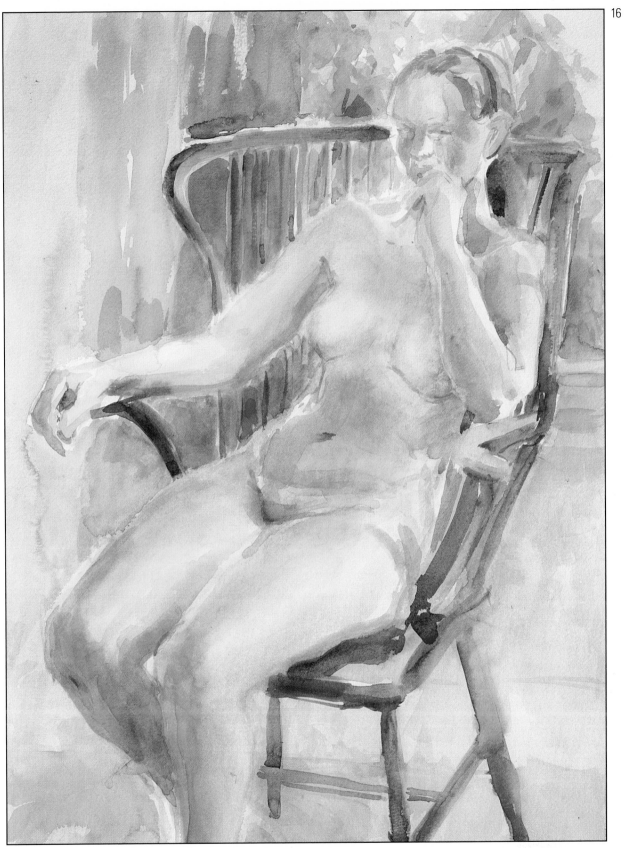

16 This whole process shows how to build up a watercolor slowly. Let the layers of paint dry thoroughly if you are going to apply a glaze over the top. It is possible by damping, sponging, and blotting to make quite drastic changes to your work.

DIFFERENT EFFECTS USING WATERCOLOR GLAZE

These five paintings are all demonstrations of the use of the watercolor glaze technique, showing how it can be used to achieve very different results.

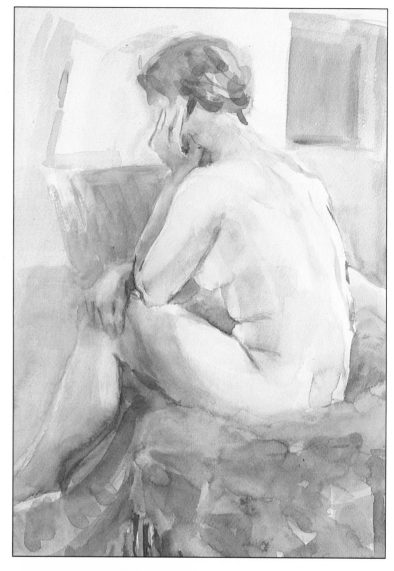

RIGHT In this watercolor of the back of a seated figure, the artist, Sharon Finmark, used exactly the same technique as in the preceding sequence. A very restricted palette – burnt sienna and cadmium yellow for the warmer areas, and a French ultramarine with a touch of viridian green glazed over thinly to delineate the planes – was used effectively to give a sense of volume.

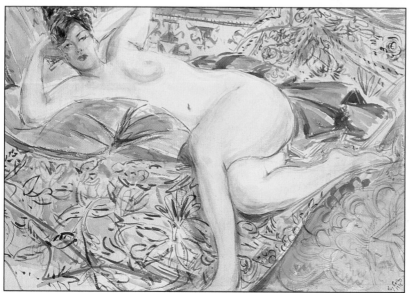

LEFT In this extravagantly posed nude, the artist, Kay Gallwey, has concentrated on building up the pattern of the drapery with thin glaze marks of different colors on top of each other, allowing the buff paper to unify the whole. In the lower right, a light sepia glaze right across the pattern brings it together. Simple linear drawing in the figure has allowed the use of one or two rhythmical glazes of light crimson along the form, leaving the paper to describe the bulk of the warm flesh.

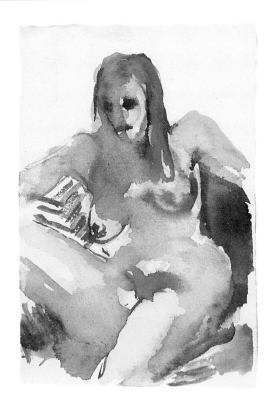

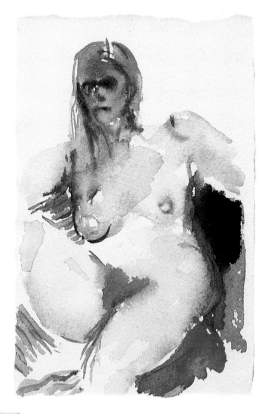

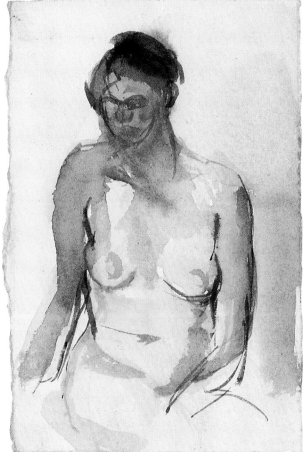

ABOVE The simplest of means has been used in the two small, rapid studies by the author of a ginger-haired girl. One or two glazes of cool and warm colors describe the form. The smaller of the two shows glazes bleeding into each other, which is not unwelcome.

LEFT Mainly French ultramarine with a touch of alizarin crimson has been glazed over cadmium yellow in this torso by the author. Virtually only two glazes have been used, with a little linear work. Constant rapid experiments with watercolor are necessary to preserve the medium's unique qualities of luminosity.

16

WET-INTO-WET WATERCOLOR

Working wet into wet, that is applying new paint while the previous paint is still wet, is an extension of the watercolor glaze technique. It is possible to exploit and to some extent control the behaviour of the paint as each new mark bleeds into the next, because the degree of bleeding depends on the dampness of the paper. As the paint dries glazing will occur anyway, and by working rapidly you will build up a rich and lively paint surface.

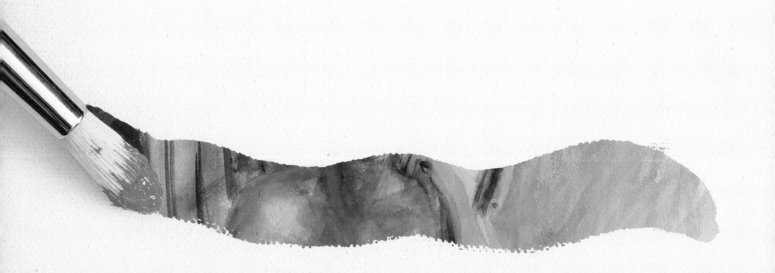

GIRL SITTING IN A WOODEN CHAIR

D A V I D   C A R R

The palette is French ultramarine, cerulean blue (mountain blue), cobalt green light, cobalt green dark, viridian green, Hooker's green, *stil de grain* vert (green-pink), cadmium yellow light, cadmium yellow deep, pozzouli earth, cadmium red light, cadmium red deep, and ultramarine violet.

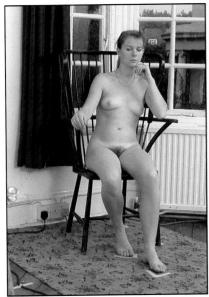

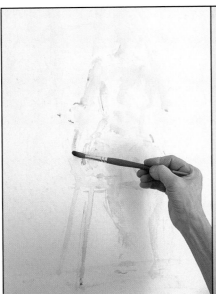

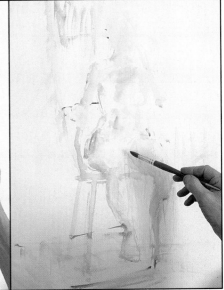

1 This is exactly the same pose as that in the previous sequence on page 105, but viewed from a new angle.

2 Dipping a large sable brush in clear water, the artist takes up a slight amount of color from the pan. Cadmium yellow deep and cadmium red light are used to mass in the figure lightly. The artist is thinking in terms of mass rather than line.

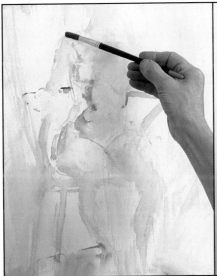

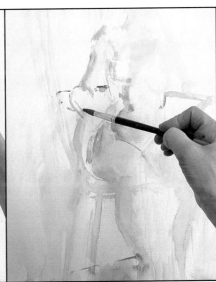

3 He then picks up some cerulean blue and cobalt green light to describe volume and to begin to define the chair. It is important to consider the chair at this stage rather than leaving it as an afterthought, hoping that it will still fit in. The paint is damp, and some slight bleeding should be allowed to occur.

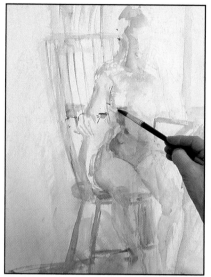

4 Keeping the paint wet, the artist now gives some attention to the model's immediate surroundings. He is not interested in detail here, but more in patches of light and shade. He begins to define the walls and floor using cadmium yellow deep (very dilute) and *stil de grain* (a warm, slightly golden color) for the light areas, cerulean blue, ultramarine and cobalt green dark for the shadows.

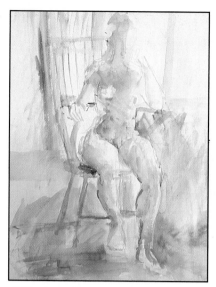

5 The form of the figure is further defined using a fairly neutral mixture of cadmium red and cobalt green deep, especially around the legs. A mixture of cadmium yellow and red gives greater strength to the torso.

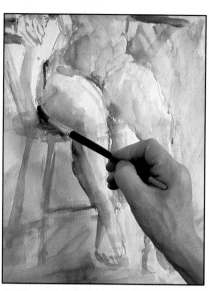

6 The model's right leg is more clearly defined by a bold stroke of cobalt green dark down the inside of the calf.

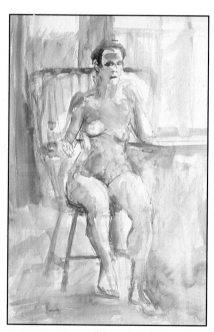

7 Taking a finer sable and a mixture of pozzouli earth and ultramarine, the artist uses some linear work to create greater clarity of form, notably under the breasts, around the thighs and in the area of the head.

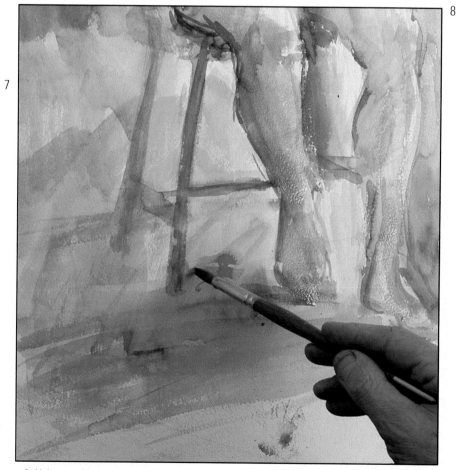

8 Using a sable brush, he applies larger areas of color to the floor and walls at the bottom of the picture and adds warmer tones to the figure's right leg.

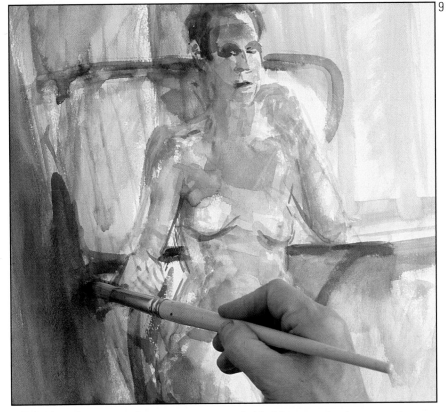

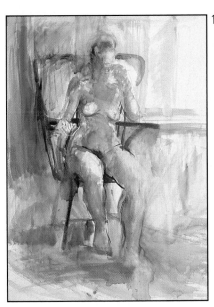

10 In order to broaden the form – it is becoming somewhat fiddly – the artist takes a large hog-hair brush and, with plenty of clear water, washes out some of the form in the head and left leg.

9 Using lots of wet paint, the artist applies even more color around the floor and wall areas. He creates further slabs of form in the figure with cadmium red deep, which is cooler than the yellow/orange areas and pushes the form back. He is not afraid of the wet paint, because as long as he does not use too much color he has ample opportunity to build up and alter the form. By now most of the earlier paint layers have dried and something of a glaze technique will operate.

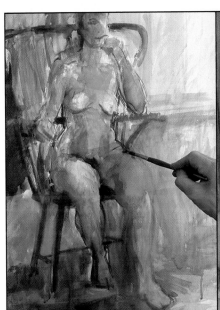

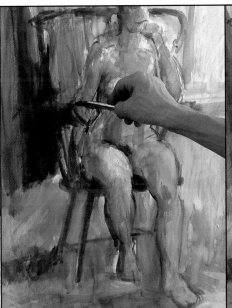

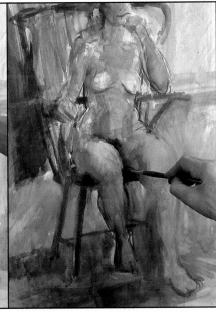

11 Using the hog-hair brush, the artist reestablishes some of this form, and redraws into it using a sable brush. He is careful to think in terms of mass first and line second: he finds the form through mass, and linear definition follows. For example, he applies a slab of cold color to the left thigh and then draws into it with a sable brush.

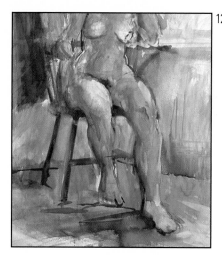

12

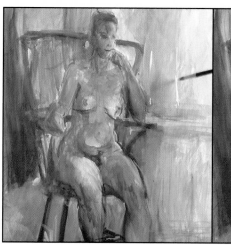

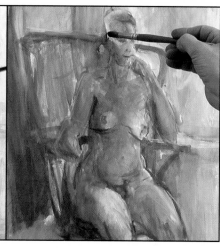

13

12 Having allowed the paint to dry a little, and consequently to lighten, he begins to define the carpet edge and floor.

13 He introduces some white body (opaque) color in gouache into the wall

area, giving a sense of light, and further defines the form of the figure.

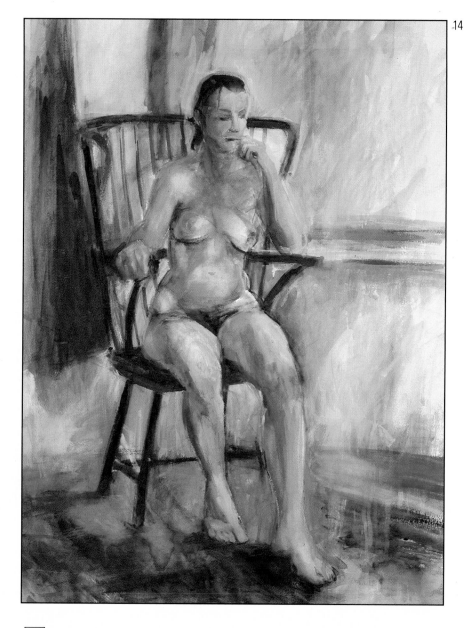

14

14 Finding that some of the color on the figure is now too heavy and is flattening the form, he takes a sponge and pulls some of this wet paint away to increase the sense of light.

17

TAKING IT FURTHER

A useful exercise and practice to keep paintings feeling fresh and spontaneous is to work on more than one painting simultaneously. This way we are likely to preserve the freshness of the initial painting that is so often lost when the picture is finished.

Take a piece of board or paper and work on one painting for a few minutes until you feel the freshness going and you are wondering what to do next. At this point begin a second picture. That will go well for a while, and when it begins to go stale look at the first picture and carry on with that and so on, working alternately on each.

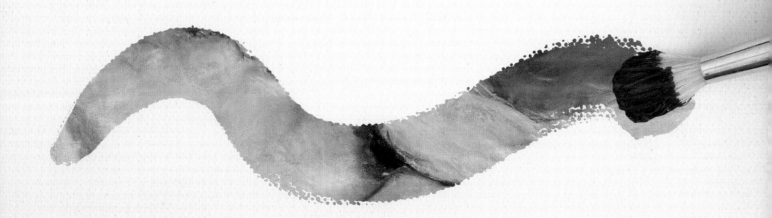

WORKING ON MORE THAN ONE IMAGE

These two small watercolors were worked on in this way. They are both
8 × 6 in (20 × 15 cm) and painted on off-white, acid-free mount board. This is an
excellent surface to work on as it will neither cockle nor chew. The palette is
French ultramarine, viridian green, cadmium lemon, cadmium yellow, cadmium
red, and white (gouache). It is in fact bordering on a gouache technique, as white
is extensively used, giving the paint body. The model is seated on the floor, and
the full figure was done first.

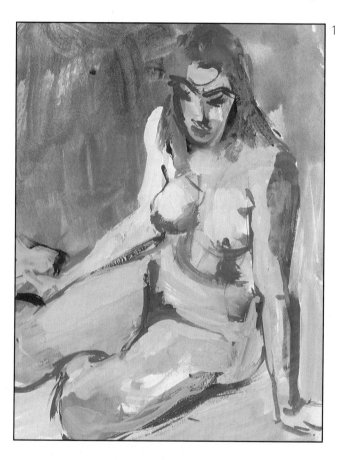

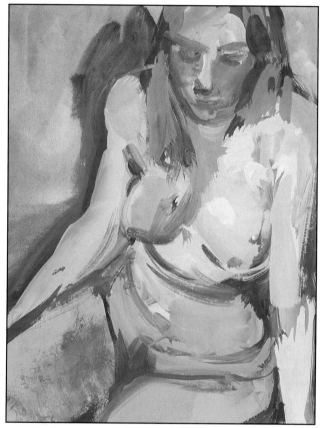

1 The gouache was applied as thinly as watercolor at first, warm and cold pinks and yellows being used for the flesh. Linear work and definition came second, with the use of a dark gray-violet (ultramarine, cadmium red, and white) and gray-green (viridian with a touch of cadmium red and white). These are complementary to the yellows and pinks. Body color is added to the model's right arm, breasts, and hair.

2 As the painting began to "die," the second picture was started, giving a stronger impression of form and the model's personality. The whole form is brought forward so that it fills the picture surface.

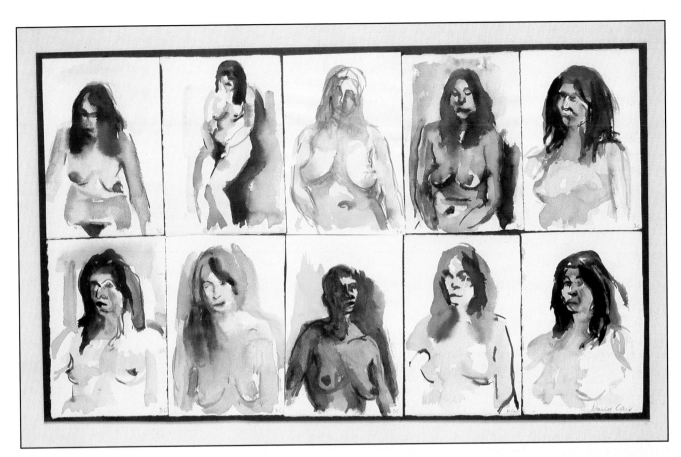

ABOVE **This series of small watercolor head-and-shoulders studies was conceived in a similar way. They are mounted together, and are examples of the same model painted in different ways, sometimes with a light glaze technique, other times with more wet into wet and with body color.**

Although the pose of these two standing figures, painted in oils, is slightly different, they were painted *alla prima* in the same evening.

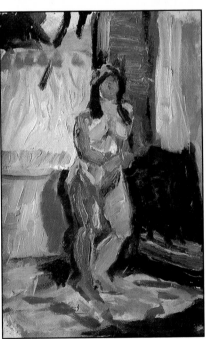

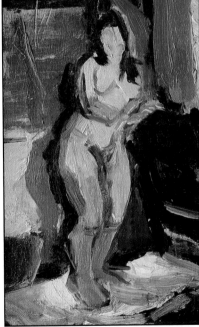

1 The first, with the figure set back a little, is a perfectly acceptable Impressionist study.

2 The second, however, has more verve and movement, and feels less fiddly. The bold primary colors around the figure and the green shadow seem more inventive, and there is a good sense of the harshness of the electric light on the upper part of the figure's torso.

MOVING INTO MIXED TECHNIQUES

Watercolor moving into gouache suggests other combinations of water-based techniques. Pure watercolor exploits the white of the paper and sometimes the color of the paper. Essentially, it is a transparent medium, and it is for these qualities that it is valued. Once "body" color is introduced, gouache techniques, which are a little more akin to those of oil paint, begin to apply. The paint can be moved around more flexibly, and free overpainting can occur. Additional techniques are possible with the introduction of other water-based materials.

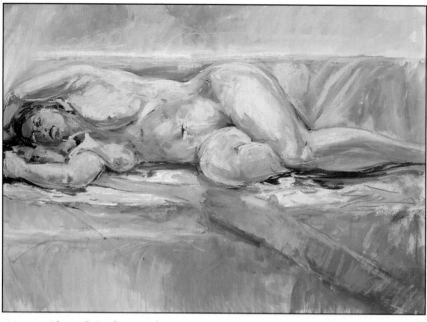

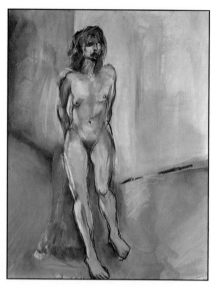

ABOVE The reclining figure with arm stretched, by the author, was begun in watercolor and gouache. All the main areas of figure and space were washed in with large brushes (in some cases oil-painting brushes). Pastel was worked into this, and fingers and brushes pushed it in to give body to the form. Pastel sticks are held together with water-soluble gum, and they can be brushed into the painting with water. In this way large areas can be covered with color. In the final stages of this painting, dry pastel was used to impart a crispness and clarity to the form.

ABOVE The almost Fauvist standing figure by the author employs the same technique. Large areas of simple space were washed in with pastel, water, and gouache. The figure was established with a light, warm yellow wash. Blue, chalky pink, and lemon yellow pastel were worked into this, and linear work was done with a dark gray chalk. Heavy drawing was worked in around the head. A final highlight down the leg was made with an eraser, pulling off some of the dense color and revealing the warm ground underneath.

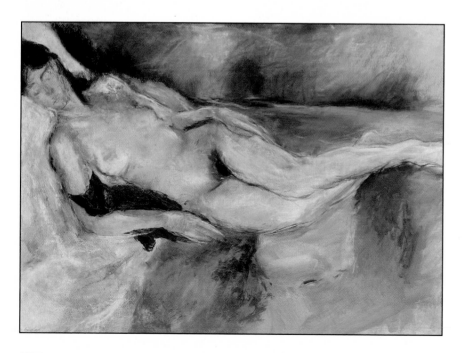

LEFT The nude holding the cat was painted by the author using yellow and pink washes of gouache and pastel. The bed was painted with large brushes. Pastel is "scumbled" over this. Where it becomes too insistent, it is washed into the surface and further layers are built up to give a translucent effect.

WORKING FROM DRAWINGS

Working from drawings is a very long-established practice. It helps to train the visual memory, and gives direction to the drawings being made. They need precision and eloquence if they are to provide sufficient information for the subsequent painting. The great Post-Impressionist painter Bonnard (1867–1947) said he felt weak in front of nature, and his practice was to make small drawings from life and relive the experience in the studio, painting the subject at a later date or time. Sickert's (1860–1942) favored working method was to make small drawings and studies of his subjects. He enlarged these for the finished painting, which was executed away from the motif.

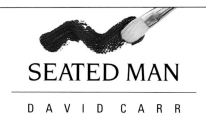

SEATED MAN

DAVID CARR

In this sequence, the artist used the technique described above. It is important to ask the questions: "Can I paint from this drawing? Does it tell me enough about the subject?" This concentrates the mind, and helps you to make clear, informative drawings. Painters often make color notes on the actual drawings to aid their memories. The palette for this painting was French ultramarine, viridian green, yellow ocher, raw sienna, cadmium red, alizarin crimson, and titanium white.

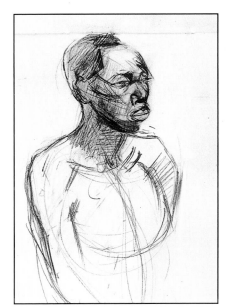

1 A careful study was made of the seated figure as well as a small drawing of the head. Quite extensive color notes have been made on the drawing as the black skin is reflecting both warm and cold light from the interior lighting and daylight.

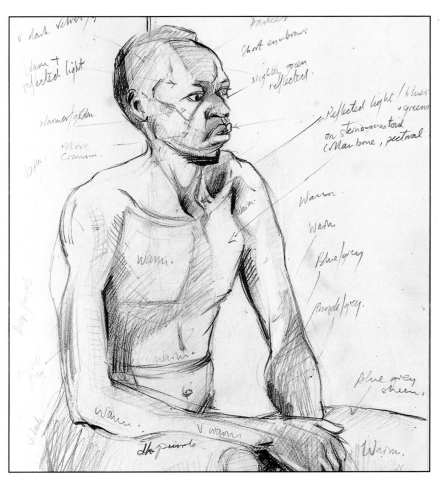

1

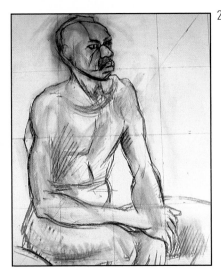

2 Having been as clear as possible about the planes in the figure, as well as the light, the artist squares up the drawing (in this case with a squared-up piece of tracing paper) and transfers it in charcoal to a larger board with the same proportions.

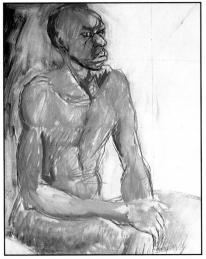

3 The figure is washed in with raw sienna and then a heavier layer of cadmium red and raw sienna. Gray-violet (mixed from alizarin crimson, French ultramarine, and raw sienna) is rubbed in for darker tones.

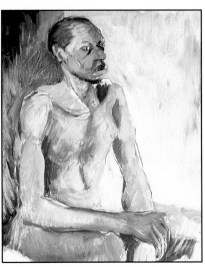

4 All this is blended together with titanium white, and a little viridian green is introduced into the chest.

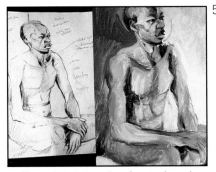

5 The artist constantly refers to the color notes on his drawing.

6 Much more work is done around the figure: the artist concentrates on the volume of the head, working wet into wet, adjusting and balancing the warm and cold light, and deciding what is reflected light and what is body color. He begins to pull it together with some yellow ocher, and a pale green reflection on the chest is established.

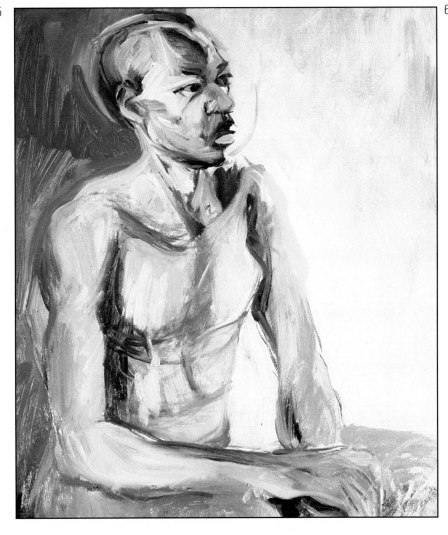

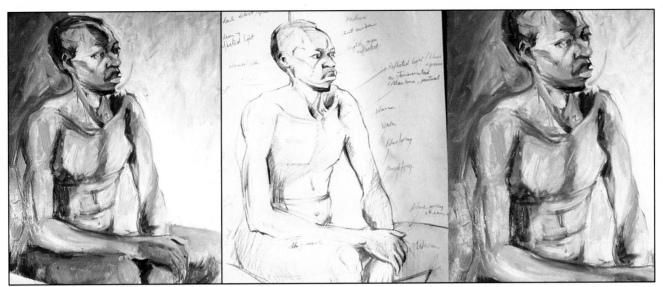

6

7 By constant reference to the drawing, the artist is gradually able to resolve the structure of the head, neck and shoulders, and build up the color in the body.

8

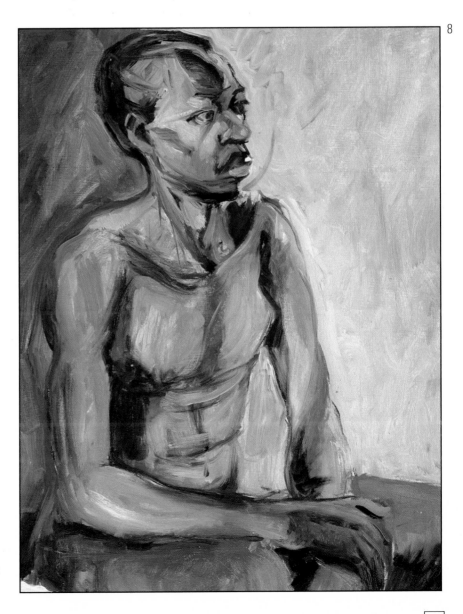

8 Practice in these techniques can enable you to make finished pictures of subjects where you have only limited time for direct study.

WORKING AT HOME

There is ample opportunity to work from the figure by joining a life-drawing class at a local art school. Tuition, advice, and contact with other painters can be invaluable.

The life room, however, can often seem artificial, although many fine paintings have been produced there. Working at home and in domestic surroundings offers a much more natural setting. The work of Bonnard (1867–1947) and Vuillard (1869–1940) springs to mind, as well as that of Sickert. Hiring a model yourself, or asking a friend to pose, can often produce more interesting images than art school studies.

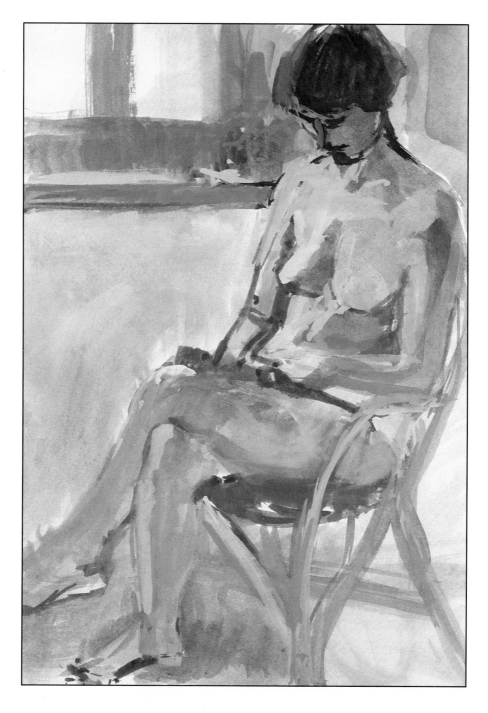

ABOVE The reading figure, painted by the author, was sitting naturally at a window. Again, there is an economy of means here. This is watercolor with added white body color. Warm orange – cadmium yellow and red – for the main body area was overlaid with thin transparent planes of the same mixture with white added. Touches of viridian in the hair and around the head helped to create a sense of light along with the cool paint on the wall.

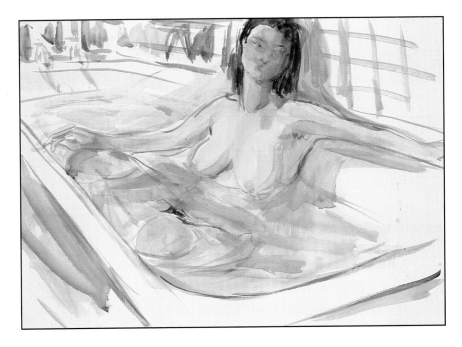

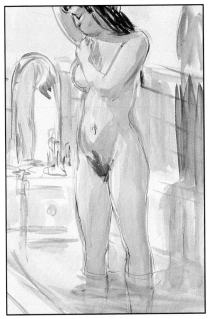

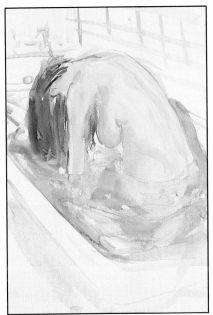

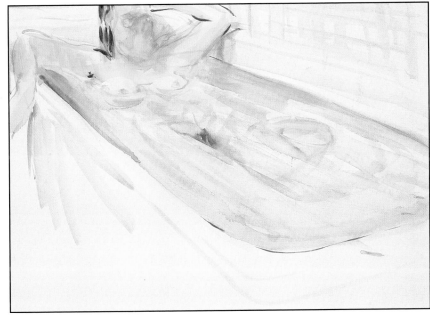

ABOVE This artist, Kay Gallwey, asked
her model to take a bath, and produced
these four fresh watercolor images using
two colors in the main, burnt sienna and
French ultramarine, with a little sap green
in the water and burnt umber to emphasize
the drawing.

LOOKING AT OTHER PAINTINGS

The persistence of themes and archetypes, of myths and legends, of the great religious subjects throughout the history of art has already been referred to. The practice of looking at other paintings and copying them is most rewarding. As well as getting to know paintings more thoroughly, you can gain an understanding of underlying compositional devices.

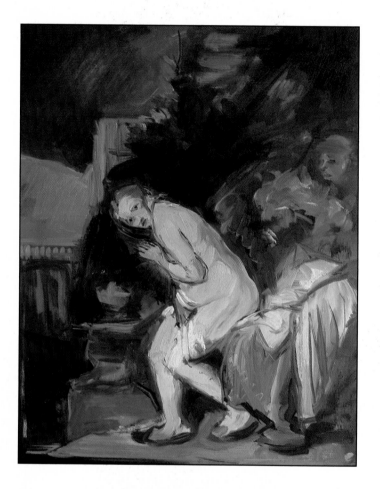

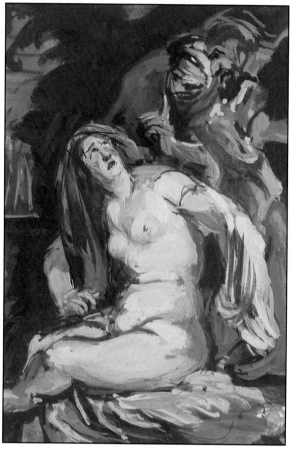

ABOVE **The story of Susanna and the Elders has exercised many a painter's imagination. In essence, two lecherous gentlemen proposition Susanna, whom they have been watching bathing for weeks. She refuses their advances, and it is ultimately only the wisdom of Daniel that saves her. It is a wonderful opportunity to contrast the naked female form with clothed figures and landscape. In a sense, Manet's *Déjeuner sur l'Herbe* of 1863 exploits the same idea, except that there the naked lady seems happy to enjoy her picnic with the gentlemen in morning dress. This small oil is a copy of one of Rembrandt's versions of the story. One elder is just discernible to the right in the bushes as Susanna clasps her clothes around her in alarm.**

ABOVE **In this small gouache copy of Rubens's treatment of the subject, the elders are much more forthright as they crowd over the fearful Susanna. As one speaks, the other ominously warns her to be silent.**

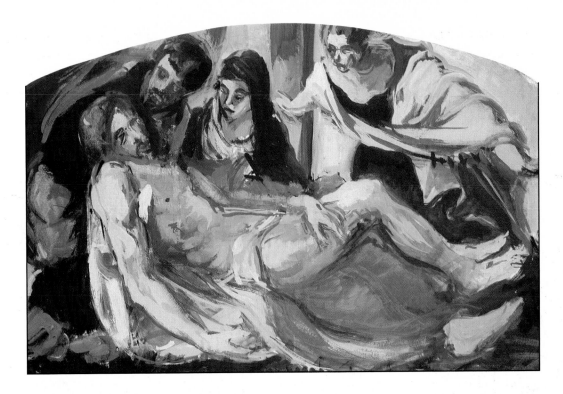

ABOVE In his painting *Pietá*, Tintoretto (1518–94) places the dead Christ at the foot of the cross in his Mother's lap as the other Mary looks on with arms outstretched. The shaped panel, the semi-circular rhythms of the body, the draperies, the arm, and Mary's shoulders echo each other in this closely knit composition. This copy was done in gouache on board.

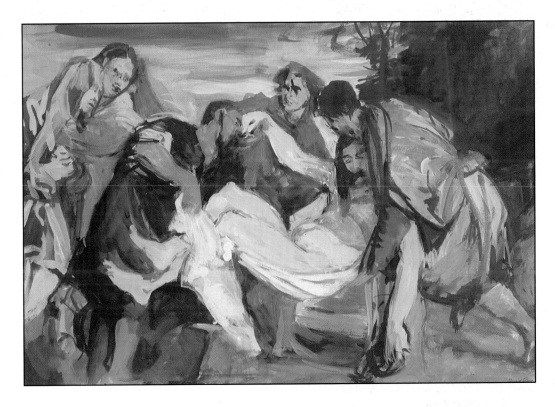

ABOVE Exploring and copying works has been carried out by all the great masters of the past. Titian's great masterpiece, *The Entombment*, in the Louvre was copied by both Delacroix (1798–1863) and Gericault (1791–1824). The composition harks back even further to a relief carved on the side of an antique sarcophagus. The disciples hold the weight of the dead Christ. The rhythmical curve of their backs and the wonderful echoed movements of the arms make a memorable composition, while the grief-stricken Marys look on. This study was painted with gouache on board.

INDEX

Page numbers in *italics* refer to illustration captions.

A

acrylic paint 98, 99, 103
acrylic primers 15
alla prima 32–9, *45, 65, 73, 81,* 98, 119
anatomy 7, 46–51
   arms, hands, and feet 61–7
   face 58–60
   head, neck, and shoulders 52–7
Arnold, John *60, 70*
artists' quality paint 12

B

binding vehicle 11
Bonnard, Pierre 10, 121, 124
brushes
   cleaning 14
   for oil painting 13, *13*
   for watercolor 16, *17*

C

canvas 14–16, *15,* 27
Carter, Susan 35–6
Cézanne, Paul 84, 86
Chaitow, Michael 98–101, *102*
Chevreul, Eugène, chemist 85, 86
colors
   and light 84–96
   range of (palette) 12, *12,* 16
   for skin 68–9, *70–3*
   see also restricted palette
color theory 9, 12, 84–7, *85–6,* 92
composition 26–31
contrapposto 48, *49*
Correggio 10
   Jupiter and Antiope 9

D

Delacroix, Eugène 9, 19, 85, 127
drawings, *see* preparatory studies

E

Egypt 7, *7*
Expressionist art 8, 10

F

Fauvism/Fauvist approach 85, 87, 92–6, *120*
figure painting 74–9
fingers, use of 37, 76–7, 91, 99, 120
Finmark, Sharon *43,* 105–9, *110*

G

Gallwey, Kay 24–5, *39, 71,* 76–7, *76,* 77, 88–91, 92–4, *110, 125*
Giacometti, Alberto 10, 74, 78
   Annette Assise 78, 78

Giorgione 10
glaze technique 32, *41–2,* 69, *70,* 96, 97–111, *119*
glue size 15–16
gouache *30,* 98, 116, 118, 120, *126, 127*
Goya, Francisco 10
   Naked Maja 9, 10
Greek art 8, 9

I

impasto 49, 70, 98, 100
Impressionism 87, 92, 98
Italian painting 9, 11, 69, 84

K

Knowles, Mike *37, 81, 103*

L

life room 10, 124
light (and color) 69, 84–96
Lightbody, Irene *72*
linseed oil 14, 16, 33, 76

M

Manet, Edouard 10, 126
   Olympia 10, *10*
Matisse, Henri 10, 85, 92
mineral spirits 14
mixed techniques 120
Modigliani, Amedeo 74, 75
Monet, Claude 12, 92
Mumford, Jill *30, 31, 43*

O

oil glaze technique 97–103
oil painting 11, 12, 20–3, 27–9, *30–1, 43–4, 49, 60, 64–7, 69–73, 76, 79, 119*
   alla prima 33–6, *37, 45, 65, 73*
   list of colors 13
oil painting materials 13–16
   brushes 13, *13*
   mediums 14
   priming 15–16
   supports (board, canvas) 14, *14,* 27

P

paint 12, 16
   artists' quality 12
   students' quality 12
palette 13
   layout of 13
palette knife 37, 49, 73
paper
   for oils 14, 15, 16
   for watercolor 17, *17, 18*
pastel *120*
Picasso, Pablo 7, 10, 12
planes 40–5, *63, 64, 66, 70, 73*
Pompeii 8, 9, 84

preparatory studies 23, 27, 30, 121–3
primers/priming 15–16

R

rags, use of *71,* 76–7, *77, 88, 92–3*
Rembrandt 9, 12, 126
   Bathsheba with King David's Letter 8, 9
Renaissance 7, 8, 69
Renoir, Auguste 9
   Woman's Torso in Sunlight 87
restricted palette 24, 33, *43,* 69, 80–3, *110*
Roman art 8, 9
Rubens, Peter Paul 9, 12, 126

S

scumbles/scumbling 32, *66,* 69, *69,* 72, 79, *102*
Sickert, Walter 121, 124
skin color and tone 68–73
space frame 27–8
Stewart, Joy 33–4
students' quality paint 12
Susanna and the Elders 126
Symonds, Judith *73*

T

Three Graces 8, *9*
Tintoretto *127*
tissue, use of 24, *25*
Titian 10, 12, 39, 98
   The Entombment 127
tonal painting 80–3
turpentine 14, 33, 70, 71, 73, 76, 92, 93

V

Van Gogh, Vincent 33, 98
Venus 7, *7,* 8, 10

W

watercolor 12, 24–5, 28, 37, *38–9, 41–2, 43, 50–1, 71, 96, 119,* 124
   brushes 16, *17*
   list of colors 16
   mixed techniques 120
   mount board surface 118
   paper 17, *17, 18*
watercolor glaze technique 104–11, *119*
wet-into-wet watercolor 33, *41–2,* 79, 112–16, *119, 122*
Willendorf Venus 7, *7*
Willis, Victor *69*
wood supports 14
working at home 124–5
Wylan, Marie *95*

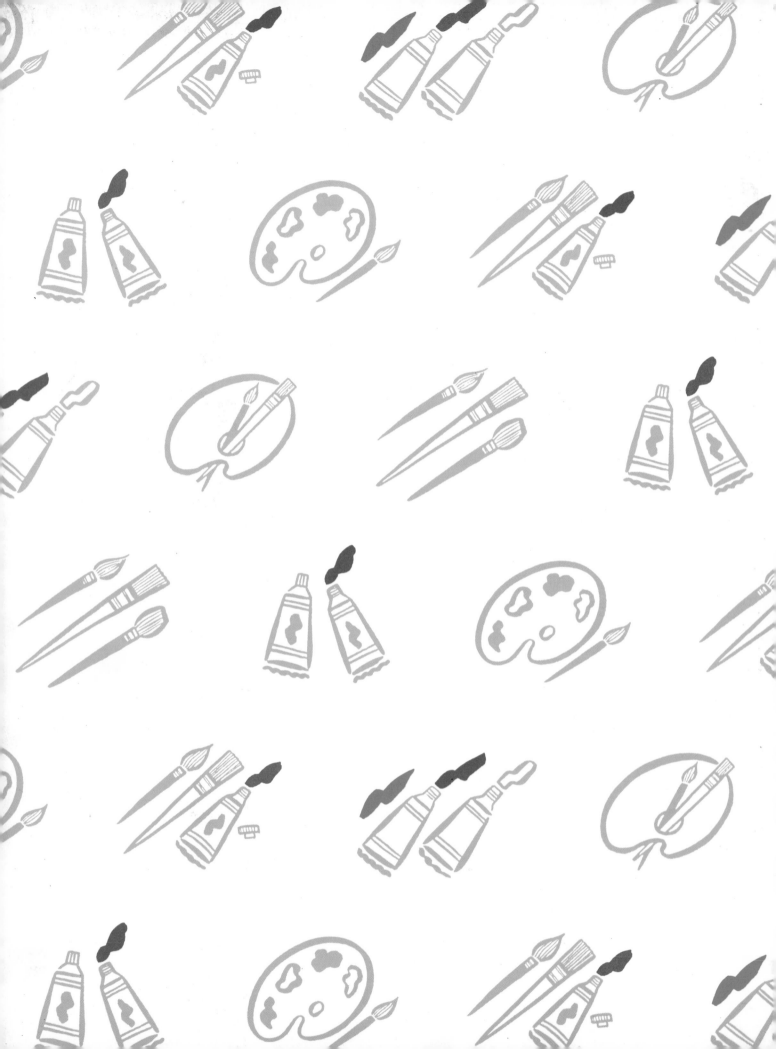